Flask By Example

Unleash the full potential of the Flask web framework
by creating simple yet powerful web applications

Gareth Dwyer

BIRMINGHAM - MUMBAI

Flask By Example

First published: March 2016

Production reference: 1220316

Published by Packt Publishing Ltd.
Livery Place
35 Livery Street
Birmingham B3 2PB, UK.

ISBN 978-1-78528-693-3

www.packtpub.com

Credits

Author
Gareth Dwyer

Reviewers
Burhan Khalid
Kyle Roux
Rahul Shelke

Commissioning Editor
Julian Ursell

Acquisition Editor
Kevin Colaco

Content Development Editor
Kajal Thapar

Technical Editors
Kunal Chaudhari
Ravikiran Pise

Copy Editors
Shruti Iyer
Sonia Mathur

Project Coordinator
Shweta H Birwatkar

Proofreader
Safis Editing

Indexer
Rekha Nair

Graphics
Disha Haria

Production Coordinator
Melwyn D'sa

Cover Work
Melwyn D'sa

About the Author

Gareth Dwyer first heard the phrase, "behind every no-entry sign there is a door," a couple of decades ago, and he has been looking for a counterexample ever since. He hasn't found one yet. Gareth grew up with his three siblings in Grahamstown, South Africa. There wasn't much there except some highly respected schools and a small university. Gareth had heard that school was an unpleasant and largely pointless experience, so he opted to skip it and go to the university instead. The university door had a no-entry sign on the door because it only accepted people who had gone to school. Gareth ignored the sign. He studied piano for a while but soon, he wondered if there was more to life than sitting in front of a keyboard all day. So he switched from piano to computer science, and it took him a while to realize the irony. He studied philosophy too because it was here that people never told him to stop being so argumentative.

Gareth noticed the disparagement that his philosophy and computer science departments felt towards each other, and he found it strange. He soon discovered that he wasn't the first person to see that there was room for some common ground, and he went to Europe to study computational linguistics, where he found other people who liked debating the finer points of language while talking about the three hardest problems of computer science (naming things, and off-by-one errors).

In between doodling on blank paper while listening to very knowledgeable people lecture on content that was occasionally fascinating but often soporific, Gareth has gained so-called "industry" experience with companies such as Amazon Web Services in Cape Town and MWR InfoSecurity in Johannesburg. He has several years' experience in writing, and his favorite languages are English and Python.

He discovered that *writing* and *writing a book* are not fullyoverlapping experiences, and the former is hardly preparation for the latter. The pages that follow would not have come into existence without the combined efforts of many people.

Acknowledgements

Thank you Neeshma and Kajal; you have been so very kind and patient in spite of my disrespect for deadlines. Your feedback on each chapter while I was writing and your suggestions that I try to keep to schedule have been invaluable. Thank you to everyone else at Packt Publishing who has been involved in this book, from its idea, through editing, through layout, through marketing, and all the nitty-gritty parts that the reader will never think about. I'm looking forward to the next one already.

Thank you Alisa for listening, even when I complained about writing, and even when I was still complaining a year later.

Thank you Theresa, Stephanie, and Lewis for ensuring I don't go completely sane.

Thank you to all the lecturers and tutors at Rhodes University who contributed to what I know and who I am.

Thank you Ron for teaching me how to string words together, and how commas work, and why some sentences sound nice and others don't.

Finally, thank you Mom and Dad for teaching me everything else.

About the Reviewers

Burhan Khalid has always been tinkering with technology, from his early days on the XT to writing JCL on the ISPF editor, and from C and C++, Java, Pascal, and COBOL to his latest favorite, Python. As a lover of technology, he is most comfortable experimenting with the next big technology stack.

By day, he works in a multinational bank in the Alternative Channels unit, where he gets to hack on, develop, and test applications that help execute transactions across all manner of electronic devices and channels. In addition to his work, he also contributes to open source projects, having released a few toolkits for transaction processing, and he offers consultancy services to startups on their technology stacks and development processes.

He is an avid volunteer; he is a mentor for Sirdab Lab (a startup accelerator), a frequent speaker at the local Google Developer's Group, a presenter and volunteer at StartupQ8 (a startup community), and an active user on StackOverflow.

You can reach him on Twitter @burhan

I would like to thank my mother and father for always encouraging me, my wife for putting up with my long days at the keyboard and my ever-growing gadget collection, and my friends and colleagues for providing me with new challenges to sharpen my skills.

Rahul Shelke is a cofounder of My Cute Office Pvt. Ltd. and Qpeka Technologies Pvt. Ltd. He also acts as an adviser for two other startups, and he helps startups in their growth.

Prior to starting his own venture, Rahul worked with Blisstering solutions for more than two years as a senior developer.

He is an MTech in computer science. His practical experience for the last five years has been in web development, cloud computing, business intelligence, system performance optimization, and software architecture design and development.

He has been actively involved in open source contributions since graduation, and he has contributed to Python, Python-Flask, and Drupal.

First, I would like to thank the Packt Publishing team, Shweta H. Birwatkar, and Gareth Dwyer, for giving me the opportunity to be a part of this project.

A special thanks to My Cute Office team whose support helped me manage work along with this book review. I would also like to thank my family for supporting me during this process.

Finally, thanks to the countless support from Python-Flask's open source community for providing me with such an easy and fast web development framework.

www.PacktPub.com

eBooks, discount offers, and more

Did you know that Packt offers eBook versions of every book published, with PDF and ePub files available? You can upgrade to the eBook version at www.PacktPub. com and as a print book customer, you are entitled to a discount on the eBook copy. Get in touch with us at customercare@packtpub.com for more details.

At www.PacktPub.com, you can also read a collection of free technical articles, sign up for a range of free newsletters and receive exclusive discounts and offers on Packt books and eBooks.

https://www2.packtpub.com/books/subscription/packtlib

Do you need instant solutions to your IT questions? PacktLib is Packt's online digital book library. Here, you can search, access, and read Packt's entire library of books.

Why subscribe?

- Fully searchable across every book published by Packt
- Copy and paste, print, and bookmark content
- On demand and accessible via a web browser

To Ron Hall, who taught me how to write

Table of Contents

Preface

In theory, nothing works, but everyone knows why. In practice, everything works but no one knows why. Here, we combine theory and practice; nothing works and no one knows why!

Learning computer science must always be a combination of theory and practice; you need to know what you're doing (theory), but you also need to know how to do it (practice). My experience of learning how to create web applications was that few teachers found a sweet spot for this balance; either I read pages and pages about inheritance, virtual environments, and test-driven development, wondering how it all applied to me, or I installed a bunch of tools and frameworks and libraries and watched the magic happen with no idea how it worked.

What follows is, I hope, a good balance. From the first chapter, you'll have a Flask web application running that the whole world can visit, which is quite practical even if it doesn't do anything but greet visitors with "Hello, World!". In the chapters that follow, we'll walk through building three interesting and useful projects together. In general, we'll build things ourselves wherever possible. While it's not good to reinvent the wheel, it is good to be exposed to a problem before you're exposed to the solution. Learning a CSS framework before you write a single line of CSS leaves you in a confused state, in which you would wonder, "But why do I actually need this?", and the same goes for many other frameworks and tools. So, we'll start from scratch, take a look at why it's difficult, and then introduce tools to make our lives easier. I think this is the ideal balance between theory and practice.

When I told people I was writing a book on Flask, the common response was "Why? There are already so many books and tutorials on Flask." This is a valid question, and the answer to it provides a nice outline for what to expect from this book. *Flask By Example* is different from other Flask educational material and here's why.

We won't leave you stranded

Many Flask tutorials show you how to develop a Flask application and run it locally on your own machine, and then they end. This is great as a first step, but if you're interested in building web applications, you probably want them to be accessible on the Web so that your friends, family, coworkers, and customers can admire your handiwork without popping by your house. From our first project onward, our applications will run on a Virtual Private Server (VPS) and be accessible to the world.

We won't build a blogging application

If you've read any web application development tutorials, you must have noticed that nearly every one of them is about how to build a blog using x and y. I'm pretty tired of the blog example (actually, I never want to see anyone show me how to build a blog again). Instead, you'll create some interesting, original, and possibly even useful projects while learning how to develop web applications with Flask.

We will focus on security

Cybercrime has become something of a buzzword of late. Arguably, the reason that we read about major web applications being hacked on an almost daily basis is because so many developers do not know about SQL Injection, CSRF, XSS, how to store passwords, and so many other things that should really be considered basic knowledge. As we develop the three projects in this book, we'll take the time to explain some core security concepts in detail and show you how to harden our applications against potentially malicious attackers.

We will give in-depth explanations

We won't just give you some code and tell you to run it. Wherever possible, we will explain what we're doing, why we're doing it, and how we're doing it. This means that you'll be able to take ideas from all of the projects, combine them with your own ideas, and get started with building original content right after working through this book.

Therefore, I hope that this book will be of use to you, no matter whether you are beginning to cut your teeth in the world of computer science and programming or have a computer science degree from a famous university and have compiler theory pouring out of your ears but now want to build something practical and fun. May you have as much fun working through the projects as I did while putting them together!

What this book covers

Chapter 1, Hello, World!, teaches you to set up our development environment and a web server and write our first Flask application.

Chapter 2, Getting Started with Our Headlines Project, shows you how to run Python code when the user visits a URL and how to return basic data to the user. We will also look at fetching the latest headlines automatically using RSS feeds.

Chapter 3, Using Templates in Our Headlines Project, introduces Jinja templates and integrates them into our Headlines project. We will show how to serve dynamic HTML content by passing data from our Python code to template files.

Chapter 4, User Input for Our Headlines Project, shows how to get input from our users over the Internet and use this input to customize what we will show our users. We will look at how to access currenct weather information through JSON APIs and include this information in our Headlines project.

Chapter 5, Improving the User Experience of Our Headlines Project, instructs you to add cookies to our Headlines project so that our application can remember our users' choices. We will also style our application by adding some basic CSS.

Chapter 6, Building an Interactive Crime Map, introduces our new project, which is a crime map. We will introduce relational databases, install MySQL on our server, and look at how to interact with our database from our Flask application.

Chapter 7, Adding Google Maps to our Crime Map Project, instructs you on adding a Google Maps widget and shows how to add and remove markers from the map based on our database. We will add an HTML form with various inputs for users to submit new crimes and also display the existing crimes.

Chapter 8, Validating User Input in Our Crime Map Project, polishes off our second project by making sure that users can't break it accidentally or through maliciously crafted input.

Chapter 9, Building a Waiter Caller App, introduces our final project, which is an application to call a waiter to the table at a restaurant. We will introduce Bootstrap and set up a basic User Account Control system that uses Bootstrap as the frontend.

Chapter 10, Template Inheritance and WTForms in Waiter Caller Project, introduces Jinja's template inheritance features so that we can add similar pages without duplicating code. We will use the WTForms library to make our web forms easier to build and validate.

Chapter 11, Using MongoDB with Our Waiter Caller Project, discusses how to install and configure MongoDB on our server and links it to our Waiter Caller project. We will finish off our final project by adding indices to our database and a favicon to our application.

Appendix, A Sneak Peek into the Future, outlines some important topics and technologies that we weren't able to cover in detail and gives pointers on where more can be learned about these.

What you need for this book

All the examples we will use assume that you use the Ubuntu operating system on your development machine and that you have access to a server that runs Ubuntu Server (we will discuss how to set the latter up in the first chapter). If you strongly prefer another operating system and already have a Python environment set up (including the Python package manger pip), then the examples will be easily translatable.

All other software and libraries used in the book are freely available, and we will demonstrate how to install and configure them in detail as the need arises.

Who this book is for

Have you looked at PHP and hated the clunky bloated syntax? Or, have you looked at .Net and wished that it was more open and flexible? Have you tried your hand at GUI libraries in Python and found them hard to use? If your answer to any one of these questions is yes, then this is just the book for you.

It is also intended for people who know the basics of Python and want to learn how to use it to build powerful solutions with a web frontend.

Conventions

In this book, you will find a number of text styles that distinguish between different kinds of information. Here are some examples of these styles and an explanation of their meaning.

Code words in text, database table names, folder names, filenames, file extensions, pathnames, dummy URLs, user input, and Twitter handles are shown as follows: "We can include other contexts through the use of the `include` directive."

A block of code is set as follows:

```
@app.route("/")
def get_news():
    return "no news is good news"
```

When we wish to draw your attention to a particular part of a code block, the relevant lines or items are set in bold:

```
import feedparserfrom flask import Flask
app = Flask(__name__)BBC_FEED = "http://feeds.bbci.co.uk/news/rss.xml"
```

Any command-line input or output is written as follows:

```
sudo apt-get update
sudo apt-get install git
```

New terms and **important words** are shown in bold. Words that you see on the screen, for example, in menus or dialog boxes, appear in the text like this: "Clicking the **Next** button moves you to the next screen."

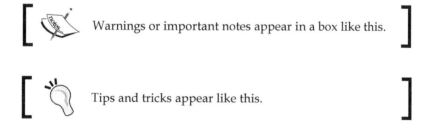

Warnings or important notes appear in a box like this.

Tips and tricks appear like this.

Reader feedback

Feedback from our readers is always welcome. Let us know what you think about this book—what you liked or disliked. Reader feedback is important for us as it helps us develop titles that you will really get the most out of.

To send us general feedback, simply e-mail feedback@packtpub.com, and mention the book's title in the subject of your message.

If there is a topic that you have expertise in and you are interested in either writing or contributing to a book, see our author guide at www.packtpub.com/authors.

Customer support

Now that you are the proud owner of a Packt book, we have a number of things to help you to get the most from your purchase.

Downloading the example code

You can download the example code files for this book from your account at http://www.packtpub.com. If you purchased this book elsewhere, you can visit http://www.packtpub.com/support and register to have the files e-mailed directly to you.

You can download the code files by following these steps:

1. Log in or register to our website using your e-mail address and password.
2. Hover the mouse pointer on the **SUPPORT** tab at the top.
3. Click on **Code Downloads & Errata**.
4. Enter the name of the book in the **Search** box.
5. Select the book for which you're looking to download the code files.
6. Choose from the drop-down menu where you purchased this book from.
7. Click on **Code Download**.

Once the file is downloaded, please make sure that you unzip or extract the folder using the latest version of:

- WinRAR / 7-Zip for Windows
- Zipeg / iZip / UnRarX for Mac
- 7-Zip / PeaZip for Linux

Downloading the color images of this book

We also provide you with a PDF file that has color images of the screenshots/diagrams used in this book. The color images will help you better understand the changes in the output. You can download this file from https://www.packtpub.com/sites/default/files/downloads/FlaskByExample_ColorImages.pdf.

Errata

Although we have taken every care to ensure the accuracy of our content, mistakes do happen. If you find a mistake in one of our books—maybe a mistake in the text or the code—we would be grateful if you could report this to us. By doing so, you can save other readers from frustration and help us improve subsequent versions of this book. If you find any errata, please report them by visiting http://www.packtpub. com/submit-errata, selecting your book, clicking on the **Errata Submission Form** link, and entering the details of your errata. Once your errata are verified, your submission will be accepted and the errata will be uploaded to our website or added to any list of existing errata under the Errata section of that title.

To view the previously submitted errata, go to https://www.packtpub.com/books/ content/support and enter the name of the book in the search field. The required information will appear under the **Errata** section.

Piracy

Piracy of copyrighted material on the Internet is an ongoing problem across all media. At Packt, we take the protection of our copyright and licenses very seriously. If you come across any illegal copies of our works in any form on the Internet, please provide us with the location address or website name immediately so that we can pursue a remedy.

Please contact us at copyright@packtpub.com with a link to the suspected pirated material.

We appreciate your help in protecting our authors and our ability to bring you valuable content.

Questions

If you have a problem with any aspect of this book, you can contact us at questions@packtpub.com, and we will do our best to address the problem.

1
Hello, World!

And hello, reader! Let's get started with building some Flask applications. Flask is minimalist enough to allow you choice and flexibility; unlike in larger frameworks, you choose what you want to do and then manipulate Flask to do your bidding, and it is complete enough to work right out of the box.

We'll walk together through the development of three web applications; the first one is straightforward and will allow you to cut your teeth on Flask and get used to the new technologies and terminology while building a nontrivial web application; the second will get you started with building a web application that makes use of a traditional SQL database; and the final, which has the most features, will make use of a **NoSQL** database and a frontend framework to create a useful and good-looking web application.

In this chapter, we'll take a brief look at what Flask is and, perhaps more importantly, what it isn't. We'll move on to setting up our basic development environment as well as a web server, and we'll install a Python package manager as well as Flask itself. By the end of the chapter, we'll have the outlines of our first app, and, as dictated by age-old tradition, we'll use our new skills to display the text "Hello, World!".

In brief, we will cover the following topics:

- Introducing Flask
- Creating our development environment
- Writing "Hello, World!"
- Deploying our application to production

Introducing Flask

Flask is a micro framework for Python web development. A framework, in the simplest terms, is a library or collection of libraries that aims to solve a part of a generic problem instead of a complete specific one. When building web applications, there are some problems that will always need to be solved, such as routing from URLs to resources, inserting dynamic data into HTML, and interacting with an end user.

Flask is a micro framework because it implements only core functionality (including routing) but leaves more advanced functionality (including authentication and database ORMs) to extensions. The result of this is less initial setup for the first-time user and more choice and flexibility for the experienced user. This is in contrast with "fuller" frameworks, such as **Django**, which dictate their own ORM and authentication technologies.

As we'll discuss, our Hello World application in Flask can be written in only seven lines of code, with the entire application consisting of a single file. Does that sound good? Let's get going!

Creating our development environment

A development environment consists of all the software that a developer uses while building software. For starters, we'll install a Python package manager (**pip**) and the Flask package. In this book, we'll show detailed steps for developing using **Python 2.7** on a clean installation of **Ubuntu 14.04**, but everything should be easy to translate to Windows or OS X.

Installing pip

For our Hello World application, we only need the Python Flask package, but we'll install several Python packages throughout the development process of our three applications. To manage these packages, we'll use the Python package manager pip. If you've developed in Python without a package manager until now, you'll love how easy it is to download, install, remove, and update packages using pip. If you already use it, then skip to the next step where we'll use it to install Flask.

The pip manager is included in Python's 3.4+ and 2.7.9+ versions. For older versions of Python, pip needs to be installed. To install pip on Ubuntu, open a terminal and run the following command:

```
sudo apt-get update
sudo apt-get install python-pip
```

To install pip on Windows or OS X, you can download and run the `get-pip.py` file from the pip homepage at `https://pip.pypa.io/en/latest/installing/#install-or-upgrade-pip`.

That's it! You can now easily install any Python package you need through pip.

Installing Flask

Installing Flask through pip could not be more straightforward. Simply run the following:

```
pip install --user flask
```

You might see some warnings in your terminal, but at the end, you should also see **Successfully installed Flask**. Now, you can import Flask into a Python program just as with any other library.

 If you're used to using VirtualEnv for Python development, you can install Flask inside a VirtualEnv environment. We will discuss this further in *Appendix, A Sneak Peek into the Future*.

Writing "Hello, World!"

Now, we'll create a basic web page and serve it using Flask's built-in server to `localhost`. This means that we'll run a web server on our local machine that we can easily make requests to from our local machine. This is very useful for development but not suited for production applications. Later on, we'll take a look at how to serve Flask web applications using the popular Apache web server.

Writing the code

Our application will be a single Python file. Create a directory in your home directory called `firstapp` and a file inside this called `hello.py`. In the `hello.py` file, we'll write code to serve a web page comprising the static string "Hello, World!". The code looks as follows:

```
from flask import Flask

app = Flask(__name__)
```

```
@app.route("/")
def index():
    return "Hello, World!"

if __name__ == '__main__':
    app.run(port=5000, debug=True)
```

Downloading the example code

You can download the example code files for this book from your account at `http://www.packtpub.com`. If you purchased this book elsewhere, you can visit `http://www.packtpub.com/support` and register to have the files e-mailed directly to you.

You can download the code files by following these steps:

- Log in or register to our website using your e-mail address and password.
- Hover the mouse pointer on the SUPPORT tab at the top.
- Click on Code Downloads & Errata.
- Enter the name of the book in the Search box.
- Select the book for which you're looking to download the code files.
- Choose from the drop-down menu where you purchased this book from.
- Click on Code Download.

Once the file is downloaded, please make sure that you unzip or extract the folder using the latest version of:

- WinRAR / 7-Zip for Windows
- Zipeg / iZip / UnRarX for Mac
- 7-Zip / PeaZip for Linux

Let's break down what this does. The first line should be familiar; it simply imports Flask from the package `flask`. The second line creates an instance of the Flask object using our module's name as a parameter. Flask uses this to resolve resources, and in complex cases, one can use something other than __name__ here. For our purposes, we'll always use __name__, which links our module to the Flask object.

Line 3 is a Python decorator. Flask uses decorators for URL routing, so this line of code means that the function directly below it should be called whenever a user visits the main *root* page of our web application (which is defined by the single forward slash). If you are not familiar with decorators, these are beautiful Python shortcuts that seem a bit like black magic at first. In essence, they call a function that takes the function defined under the decorator (in our case, `index()`) and returns a modified function.

The next two lines should also seem familiar. They define a very simple function that returns our message. As this function is called by Flask when a user visits our application, the return value of this will be what is sent in response to a user who requests our landing page.

Line 6 is a Python idiom with which you are probably familiar. This is a simple conditional statement that evaluates to True if our application is run directly. It is used to prevent Python scripts from being unintentionally run when they are imported into other Python files.

The final line kicks off Flask's development server on our local machine. We set it to run on port 5000 (we'll use port 80 for production) and set debug to True, which will help us see detailed errors directly in our web browser.

Running the code

To run our development web server, simply fire up a terminal and run the hello.py file. If you used the same structure outlined in the previous section, the commands will be as follows:

```
cd firstapp/hello
python hello.py
```

You should get an output similar to that in the following screenshot:

```
flask@ubuntu: ~/firstapp
flask@ubuntu:~$ cd firstapp/
flask@ubuntu:~/firstapp$ python hello.py
 * Running on http://127.0.0.1:5000/ (Press CTRL+C to quit)
 * Restarting with stat
```

Also, you should see the process continue to run. This is our web server listening for requests. So, let's make a request!

Fire up a web browser — I use Firefox, which comes packaged with Ubuntu — and navigate to localhost:5000.

The localhost part of the URL is a shortcut to the loopback address, usually 127.0.0.1, which asks your computer to make the web request to itself. The number after the colon (5000) is the port it should make the request to. By default, all HTTP (web) traffic is carried over port 80. For now, we'll use 5000 as it is unlikely to conflict with any existing services, but we'll change over to port 80 in production, which is conventional, so that you won't have to worry about the colon.

You should see the "Hello, World!" string displayed in your browser as in the following screenshot. Congratulations, you've built your first web application using Flask!

Deploying our application to production

It's great to have an application that runs, but inherent to the idea of a web application is the idea that we want others to be able to use it. As our application is Python-based, we are a bit limited in how we can run our application on a web server (many traditional web hosts are only configured to run PHP and/or .NET applications). Let's consider how to serve Flask applications using a **Virtual Private Server** (**VPS**) running Ubuntu Server, Apache, and WSGI.

From this point on, we'll maintain *two* environments. The first is our **development** environment, which we just set up and where we'll write code and view its results using the Flask server running on localhost (as we just did). The second will be a **production** environment. This will be a server to which we can deploy our web applications and make them accessible to the world. When we install new Python libraries or other software on our development environment, we'll normally want to mirror our actions in the production environment.

Setting up a Virtual Private Server

Although you could, in theory, host your web application on your local machine and allow others to use it, this has some severe limitations. First of all, every time you turned off your computer, your app would not be available. Also, your computer probably connects to the Internet via an Internet Service Provider (ISP) and possibly a wireless router. This means that your IP address is dynamic and changes regularly, which makes it difficult for your applications' users to keep up! Finally, chances are that you have an asymmetrical connection to the Internet, which means that your upload speed is slower than your download speed.

Hosting your application on a server solves all of these problems. Before "the cloud" became popular, the traditional way to host a web application was to buy a physical server and find a data center to host it. These days, things are far simpler. In a few minutes, you can fire up a virtual server, which to you seems just like a physical server—you can log in to it, configure it, and enjoy full control over it—but it is actually just a virtual "piece" of a machine owned and controlled by a cloud provider.

At the time of writing, major players in the cloud provider field include Amazon Web Services, Microsoft Azure, Google Cloud Compute, and Digital Ocean. All of these companies allow you to hire a virtual server or servers upon paying by the hour. If you are learning Flask as a hobby and are unwilling to pay anyone to host your web applications, you'll probably find a free trial at one of the providers quite easily. The smallest offering by any provider is fine to host all the applications that we'll run.

Select one of the preceding providers or another of your choosing. If you've never done anything similar before, Digital Ocean is often cited to have the simplest process of signing up and creating a new machine. Once you select a provider, you should be able to follow their respective instructions to fire up a VPS that runs Ubuntu Server 14.04 and SSH into it. You'll have full control over the machine with one slight difference: you won't have a display or a mouse.

You'll enter commands on your local terminal, which will in fact be run on the remote machine. Detailed instructions on how to connect to your VPS will be given by the provider, but if you use Ubuntu, it should be as simple as running the following:

```
ssh user@123.456.789.000
```

Alternatively, if you set it up with a public-private key authentication, where `yourkey.pem` is the full path to your private key file, here's the command to run:

```
ssh user@123.456.78.000 -i yourkey.pem
```

Here, `user` is the default user on the VPS, and `yourkey` is the name of your private key file.

SSH from other operating systems:

SSH from OS X should be the same as Ubuntu, but if you're using Windows, you'll have to download PuTTY. Refer to `http://www.putty.org/` to download and for full usage instructions. Note that if you use key files for authentication, you'll have to convert them to a format compatible with PuTTY. A conversion tool can also be found on the PuTTY website.

Once we connect to the VPS, installing Flask is the same process as it was previously:

```
sudo apt-get update
sudo apt-get install python-pip
pip install --user Flask
```

To install our web server, Apache, and WSGI, we will run the following:

```
sudo apt-get install apache2
sudo apt-get install libapache2-mod-wsgi
```

Apache is our web server. It will listen for web requests (which are generated by our users visiting our web application using their browsers) and hand these requests over to our Flask application. As our application is in Python, we also need **WSGI (Web Server Gateway Interface)**.

This is a common interface between web servers and Python applications, which allows Apache to talk to Flask and vice versa. An overview of the architecture can be seen in the following diagram:

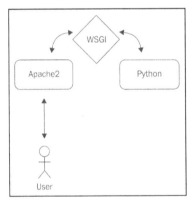

Configuring our server

Now that we've installed Apache, we can see our first results. You're probably used to visiting websites using a URL, such as http://example.com. We'll access our web applications using the IP address of our VPS directly. Your VPS should have a static public address. Static means that it doesn't change periodically, and public means that it is globally unique. When you connected to the VPS via SSH, you probably used the public IP to do this. If you can't find it, run the following on your VPS and you should see an inet addr section in the output, which contains your public IP:

```
ifconfig
```

The IP address should look similar to `123.456.78.9`. Enter your IP address into your browser's address bar, and you should see a page saying "**Apache2 Ubuntu Default Page: It Works!**" or something similar, as in the following screenshot:

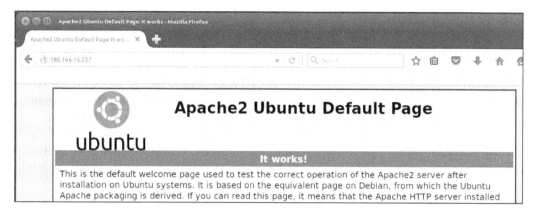

This means that we can now serve web content to anyone with an Internet connection! However, we still have to:

- Copy our code to the VPS
- Link up Apache and Flask
- Configure Apache to serve our Flask application

For the first step, we'll set up a Git repository on our local machine and clone the repository to the VPS. For the second step, we'll use the WSGI module that we installed with Apache. Finally, we'll take a look at how to write a virtual host to have Apache serve our Flask application by default.

Installing and using Git

Git is a version control system. A version control system, among other things, saves multiple versions of our code base automatically. This is great to undo accidental changes or even deletions; we can simply revert to a previous version of our code. It also includes lots of functionality for distributed development—that is, many developers working on a single project. We'll use it mainly for its backup and deployment features, however.

To install Git on your local machine and VPS, run the following commands on each:

```
sudo apt-get update
sudo apt-get install git
```

Make sure you're comfortable with the difference between running commands on your own machine using the terminal and on your server through the SSH connection. In many cases, we'll need to run the same commands twice — once for each environment.

Now that you have the software, you need a place to host your Git repositories or "repos". Two popular and free Git hosting services are GitHub (`http://github.com`) and Bitbucket (`http://bitbucket.org`). Head over to one of them, create an account, and create a new repository by following the instructions that they provide. When given the option to give your repository a name, call it `firstapp` to match the name of the directory that we will use for our code base. Once you create a new repository, you should be given a unique URL to your repository. Take note of this as we'll use it to push our **Hello, World!** application using `git` and then deploy it to our VPS.

On your local machine, open a terminal and change the directory to the Flask application. Initialize a new repository and link it to your remote Git repository via the following commands:

```
cd firstapp
git init
git remote add origin <your-git-url>
```

Tell `git` who you are, to allow it to automatically add metadata to your code changes, as follows:

```
git config --global user.email "you@example.com"
git config --global user.name "Your Name"
```

Git allows you full control over which files are part of your repository and which aren't. Even though we initialized the Git repo in our `firstapp` directory, our repo currently contains no files. Add our application to the repo, commit, and then push it, as follows:

```
git add hello.py
git commit -m "Initial commit"
git push -u origin master
```

These are the main Git commands that we'll use throughout this book, so let's take a brief look at what each does. The add command adds new or modified files to our repository. This tells Git which files are actually part of our project. Think of the commit command as taking a snapshot of our project in its current state. This snapshot is saved on our local machine. It is good to make a new commit with any major change to the code base as we can easily revert to previous commits if a later commit breaks our application. Finally, the push command pushes our local changes to the remote Git server. This is good for backup, and it will also allow us to fetch the changes on our VPS, thus keeping the code base on our local machine and that on our VPS in sync.

Now, SSH into your VPS again and get a copy of our code, as follows:

```
cd /var/www
git clone <your-git-url>
```

 Where the <your-git-url> part of the above command is actually a placeholder for the URL to your Git repository.

If you get a permission denied error on trying to clone the Git repository, you might need to take ownership of the /var/www directory for the Linux user that you're using. If you logged into the server with tom@123.456.789.123, you can run the following command, which will give your user ownership of /var/www and allow you to clone the Git repository into it. Again tom is the placeholder used in the following case:

```
sudo chown -R tom /var/www
```

If you used firstapp as a name for your remote repository, this should create a new directory called firstapp. Let's verify that our code is there using the following:

```
cd firstapp
ls
```

You should see your hello.py file. Now, we need to configure Apache to use WSGI.

Serving our Flask app with WSGI

First, we'll create a very straightforward .wsgi file in our application directory. Then, we'll create an Apache configuration file in the directory where Apache looks for available sites.

The only slightly tricky part about these two steps is that we'll create the files directly on our VPS, and as our VPS does not have a display, this means that we have to use command-line interface text editors. Of course, we could create the files locally and then transfer them to our VPS as we did for our code base, but for small changes to configuration files, this is often more effort than it's worth. Using a text editor without a mouse takes a bit of getting used to, but it's a good skill to learn. The default text editor on Ubuntu is Nano, and the other popular choices are vi or Vim. Some people use Emacs. If you already have a favorite, go with it. If not, we'll use Nano for the examples in this book (it is already installed and arguably the simplest to use). However, if you want to go the extra mile, I recommend learning to use Vim.

Assuming you're still connected to your VPS and have navigated to the /var/www/ firstapp directory as in the most recent steps, run the following command:

```
nano hello.wsgi
```

This creates the hello.wsgi file, which you can now edit through Nano. Type the following:

```
import sys
sys.path.insert(0, "/var/www/firstapp")
from hello import app as application
```

This is simply Python syntax, which patches our application into the PATH system so that Apache can find it through WSGI. We will then import app (we named this in our hello.py app with the app = Flask(__name__) line) into the namespace.

Hit *Ctrl* + *X* to exit Nano and enter *Y* when prompted to save the changes.

Now, we'll create an Apache configuration file that points to the .wsgi file we just created, as follows:

```
cd /etc/apache2/sites-available
nano hello.conf
```

> If you run into permission issues while editing or saving files, you may need to take ownership of the apache2 directory too. Run the following command, substituting the username for your Linux user:
>
> ```
> sudo chown -R tom /etc/apache2
> ```

In this file, we'll create a configuration for an Apache virtual host. This will allow us to serve multiple sites from a single server, which will be useful later when we want to serve other applications using our single VPS. In Nano, enter the following configuration:

```
<VirtualHost *>
    ServerName example.com

    WSGIScriptAlias / /var/www/firstapp/hello.wsgi
    WSGIDaemonProcess hello
    <Directory /var/www/firstapp>
       WSGIProcessGroup hello
       WSGIApplicationGroup %{GLOBAL}
        Order deny,allow
        Allow from all
    </Directory>
</VirtualHost>
```

This might look quite complicated, but it's actually very straightforward. We will create a `virtualhost` and specify our domain name, where our `.wsgi` script is, the name of our application, and who is allowed to access it. We'll discuss domain names in the final chapter, but for now, you can just leave it as `example.com` because we'll access our application by its IP address.

 If you get stuck on this step, the Flask website has a great resource on configuring and troubleshooting Apache configuration. You can find it at `http://flask.pocoo.org/docs/0.10/deploying/mod_wsgi/`.

Hit *Ctrl + X* and enter *Y* when prompted again to save and exit the file. Now, we need to enable the configuration and set it as our default site.

Configuring Apache to serve our Flask application

Apache sites work as follows: there is a `sites-available` directory (where we created the new virtual host configuration file) and a `sites-enabled` directory, which contains shortcuts to all the configuration files that we want to be active. By default, you'll see a file in the `sites-available` directory named `000-default.conf`. This is the reason that we saw a default **It works** Apache page when we first installed Apache. We don't want this anymore; instead, we want to use our application as the default site. Therefore, we'll disable the default Apache site, enable our own, and then restart Apache for the changes to take effect. Run these commands to do this:

```
sudo a2dissite 000-default.conf
sudo a2ensite hello.conf
sudo service apache2 reload
```

> The required Apache configuration and commands can vary quite a bit based on the platform you're using. If you use Ubuntu Server as recommended, the preceding should all work smoothly. If not, you may need to read up a bit on how to configure Apache for your specific platform.

You should note `reloading web server apache2` in the output. If errors are displayed, then you probably misconfigured something in the preceding command. If this is the case, read the error message carefully and go back over the previous steps to take a look at why things didn't work as expected.

To test that everything is working, open a web browser on your local machine and type your IP address into the address bar again. You should see **Hello, World!** displayed in your browser instead of the default Apache page that we saw before.

If you get **Error 500** instead, it means that our application fell over for some reason. Fear not; it's better that you get used to dealing with this error now, when the fix will probably be simple, than later on, when we've added more components that could break or be misconfigured. To find out what went wrong, run the following command on your VPS:

```
sudo tail -f /var/log/apache2/error.log
```

The `tail` command simply outputs the last several lines of the file passed as an argument. The `-f` is for follow, which means that the output will be updated if the file changes. If you can't immediately work out which lines are indicative of the error we're looking for, visit the site in your web browser on your local machine again, and you'll see the output from the `tail` command be updated accordingly. The following screenshot shows the output from the `tail` command when there are no errors; however, if anything goes wrong, you'll see the error output printed among all the info messages.

```
root@blank: ~
root@blank:~# tail -f /var/log/apache2/error.log
[Wed Mar 02 13:23:49.586889 2016] [mpm_event:notice] [pid 97
9:tid 140715828262784] AH00489: Apache/2.4.7 (Ubuntu) mod_ws
gi/3.4 Python/2.7.6 configured -- resuming normal operations
[Wed Mar 02 13:23:49.586923 2016] [core:notice] [pid 979:tid
 140715828262784] AH00094: Command line: '/usr/sbin/apache2'
[Wed Mar 02 13:23:52.141654 2016] [mpm_event:notice] [pid 97
9:tid 140715828262784] AH00493: SIGUSR1 received.  Doing gra
ceful restart
AH00558: apache2: Could not reliably determine the server's
fully qualified domain name, using 127.0.1.1. Set the 'Serve
rName' directive globally to suppress this message
[Wed Mar 02 13:23:52.194574 2016] [mpm_event:notice] [pid 97
9:tid 140715828262784] AH00489: Apache/2.4.7 (Ubuntu) mod_ws
gi/3.4 Python/2.7.6 configured -- resuming normal operations
[Wed Mar 02 13:23:52.194607 2016] [core:notice] [pid 979:tid
 140715828262784] AH00094: Command line: '/usr/sbin/apache2'
[Wed Mar 02 14:20:56.644223 2016] [mpm_event:notice] [pid 97
9:tid 140715828262784] AH00493: SIGUSR1 received.  Doing gra
ceful restart
AH00558: apache2: Could not reliably determine the server's
fully qualified domain name, using 127.0.1.1. Set the 'Serve
rName' directive globally to suppress this message
[Wed Mar 02 14:20:57.059385 2016] [mpm_event:notice] [pid 97
9:tid 140715828262784] AH00489: Apache/2.4.7 (Ubuntu) mod_ws
gi/3.4 Python/2.7.6 configured -- resuming normal operations
[Wed Mar 02 14:20:57.059449 2016] [core:notice] [pid 979:tid
 140715828262784] AH00094: Command line: '/usr/sbin/apache2'
```

Some possible tripping points are incorrectly configured WSGI and Apache files
(make sure that your `WSGIDaemonProcess` and `daemon name` match, for example) or
incorrectly configured Python (you may forget to install Flask on your VPS). If you
can't figure out what the error message means, an Internet search for the message
(removing the error-specific parts of your app, such as names and paths) will usually
point you in the right direction. Failing this, there are strong and very friendly Flask
and WSGI communities on Stack Overflow and Google Groups, and there's normally
someone willing to help beginners. Remember that if you're having a problem and
can't find an existing solution online, don't feel bad for asking; you'll help countless
people facing issues similar to yours.

Summary

We got through quite a lot of material in this first chapter! We did some initial setup and house-keeping and then wrote our first web application using Flask. We saw this run locally and then discussed how to use Git to copy our code to a server. We configured our server to serve our application to the public; however, our application is merely a static page that prints the "Hello, World!" string to whoever visits our page. This is not useful to many people and could be achieved more simply using a static HTML page. However, with the extra effort we put in, we now have all the power of Python behind our application; we're just not using it yet!

In the next chapter, we'll discover how to take advantage of Python to make our web applications more useful!

2
Getting Started with Our Headlines Project

Now that our Hello World application is up and running, we have all the groundwork in place to create a more useful application. Over the next few chapters, we'll create a Headlines application that displays up-to-date news headlines, weather information, and currency exchange rates to our users.

In this chapter, we'll introduce RSS feeds and show how to use them to automatically retrieve recent news articles from specific publications. In the next chapter, we'll discuss how to use templates to display headlines and summaries of the retrieved articles to our users. *Chapter 4, User Input for Our Headlines Page Project,* will show you how to get input from users so that they can customize their experience and will also look at how to add weather and currency data to our application. We'll finish off the project in *Chapter 5, Improving the User Experience of Our Headlines Project,* by adding some CSS styles and looking at how to remember our users' preferences from one visit to the next.

By the end of this chapter, you'll have learned how to create a more complex Flask application. We'll pull raw data from real-world news stories and build up HTML formatting to display this to our user. You'll also learn more about routing—that is, having different URLs trigger different parts of our application's code.

In this chapter, we will cover the following topics:

- Setting up our project and a Git repository
- Creating a new Flask application
- Introduction to RSS and RSS feeds

Setting up our project and a Git repository

We could simply edit our Hello World application to add the desired functionality, but it's cleaner to start a new project. We'll create a new Git repository, a new Python file, a new `.wsgi` file, and a new Apache configuration file. We'll do this for each of the projects in the book, which means that all three of the projects as well as the original Hello World application will be accessible from our web server.

Setting up is very similar to what we did for our Hello World application in *Chapter 1, Hello, World!* but we'll briefly go through the steps again as we don't have to repeat a lot of the configuration and installation, as follows:

1. Log in to your GitHub or BitBucket account and create a new repository called `headlines`. Take note of the URL you're given for this blank repository.

2. On your local machine, create a new directory called `headlines` in your home directory or wherever you put the `firstapp` directory.

3. Create a new file in this directory called `headlines.py`.

4. In your terminal, change the directory to the `headlines` directory and initialize the Git repository by executing the following commands:

```
cd headlines
git init
git remote add origin <your headlines git URL>
git add headlines.py
git commit -m "initial commit"
git push -u origin master
```

Now, we're almost ready to push code to our new repository; we just need to write it first.

Creating a new Flask application

To begin with, we'll create the skeleton of our new Flask application, which is pretty much the same as our Hello World application. Open `headlines.py` in your editor and write the following code:

```
from flask import Flask

app = Flask(__name__)
```

```
@app.route("/")
def get_news():
  return "no news is good news"

if __name__ == '__main__':
  app.run(port=5000, debug=True)
```

This works exactly as before. You can run it in your terminal with `python headlines.py`. Open a browser and navigate to `localhost:5000` to see the **no news is good news** string displayed. However, although the old adage may be true, it's bad news that our app does not do anything more useful than this. Let's make it display actual news to our users.

Introduction to RSS and RSS feeds

RSS is an old but still widely used technology to manage content feeds. It's been around for such a long time that there's some debate as to what the letters RSS actually stand for, with some saying Really Simple Syndication and others Rich Site Summary. It's a bit of a moot point as everyone just calls it RSS.

RSS presents content in an ordered and structured format using XML. It has several uses, with one of the more common uses being for people to consume news articles. On news websites, news is usually laid out similarly to a print newspaper with more important articles being given more space and also staying on the page for longer. This means that frequent visitors to the page will see some content repeatedly and have to look out for new content. On the other hand, some web pages are updated only very infrequently, such as some authors' blogs. Users have to keep on checking these pages to see whether they are updated, even when they haven't changed most of the time. RSS feeds solve both of these problems. If a website is configured to use RSS feeds, all new content is published to a feed. A user can subscribe to the feeds of his or her choice and consume these using an RSS reader. New stories from all feeds he or she has subscribed to will appear in the reader and disappear once they are marked as read.

As RSS feeds have a formal structure, they allow us to easily parse the headline, article text, and date programmatically in Python. We'll use some RSS feeds from major news publications to display news to our application's users.

Although RSS follows a strict format and we could, with not too much trouble, write the logic to parse the feeds ourselves, we'll use a Python library to do this. The library abstracts away things such as different versions of RSS and allows us to access the data we need in a completely consistent fashion.

There are several Python libraries that we could use to achieve this. We'll select `feedparser`. To install it, open your terminal and type the following:

```
pip install --user feedparser
```

Now, let's go find an RSS feed to parse! Most major publications offer RSS feeds, and smaller sites built on popular platforms, such as WordPress and Blogger, will often have RSS included by default as well. Sometimes, a bit of effort is required to find the RSS feed; however, as there is no standard as to where it should be located, you'll often see the RSS icon somewhere on the homepage (look at the headers and footers), which looks similar to this:

Also, look for links saying **RSS** or **Feed**. If this fails, try going to `site.com/rss` or `site.com/feed`, where `site.com` is the root URL of the site for which you're looking for RSS feeds.

We'll use the RSS feed for the main BBC news page. At the time of writing, it is located at `http://feeds.bbci.co.uk/news/rss.xml`. If you're curious, you can open the URL in your browser, right-click somewhere on the page, and click on **View Source** or an equivalent. You should see some structured XML with a format similar to the following:

```
<?xml version="1.0" encoding="UTF-8"?>
  <channel>
    <title>FooBar publishing</title>
    <link>http://dwyer.co.za</link>
    <description>A mock RSS feed</description>
    <language>en-gb</language>
    <item>
      <title>Flask by Example sells out</title>
      <description>Gareth Dwyer's new book,
      Flask by Example sells out in minutes</description>
      <link>http://dwyer.co.za/book/news/flask-by-example</link>
      <guid isPermalink="false">http://dwyer.co.za/book/news/
      flask-by-example</guid>
      <pubDate>Sat, 07 Mar 2015 09:09:19 GMT</pubDate>
    </item>
  </channel>
</rss>
```

At the very top of the feed, you'll see a line or two that describes the feed itself, such as which version of RSS it uses and possibly some information about the styles. After this, you'll see information relating to the publisher of the feed followed by a list of <item> tags. Each of these represents a *story*—in our case, a news article. These items contain information such as the headline, a summary, the date of publication, and a link to the full story. Let's get parsing!

Using RSS from Python

In our headlines.py file, we'll make modifications to import the feedparser library we installed, parse the feed, and grab the first article. We'll build up HTML formatting around the first article and show this in our application. If you're not familiar with HTML, it stands for **Hyper Text Markup Language** and is used to define the look and layout of text in web pages. It's pretty straightforward, but if it's completely new to you, you should take a moment now to go through a beginner tutorial to get familiar with its most basic usage. There are many free tutorials online, and a quick search should bring up dozens. A popular and very beginner-friendly one can be found at http://www.w3schools.com/html/.

Our new code adds the import for the new library, defines a new global variable for the RSS feed URL, and further adds a few lines of logic to parse the feed, grab the data we're interested in, and insert this into some very basic HTML. It looks similar to this:

```python
import feedparser

from flask import Flask

app = Flask(__name__)

BBC_FEED = "http://feeds.bbci.co.uk/news/rss.xml"


@app.route("/")
def get_news():
    feed = feedparser.parse(BBC_FEED)
    first_article = feed['entries'][0]
    return """<html>
    <body>
        <h1> BBC Headlines </h1>
        <b>{0}</b> <br/>
        <i>{1}</i> <br/>
```

```
        <p>{2}</p> <br/>
    </body>
</html>""".format(first_article.get("title"), first_article.
get("published"), first_article.get("summary"))

if __name__ == "__main__":
    app.run(port=5000, debug=True)
```

The first line of this function passes the BBC feed URL to our `feedparser` library, which downloads the feed, parses it, and returns a Python dictionary. In the second line, we grabbed just the first article from the feed and assigned it to a variable. The `entries` entry in the dictionary returned by `feedparser` contains a list of all the items that include the news stories we spoke about earlier, so we took the first one of these and got the headline or `title`, the date or the `published` field, and the summary of the article (that is, `summary`) from this. In the `return` statement, we built a basic HTML page all within a single triple-quoted Python string, which includes the `<html>` and `<body>` tags that all HTML pages have as well as an `<h1>` heading that describes what our page is; `<b>`, which is a *bold* tag that shows the news headline; `<i>`, which stands for the *italics* tag that shows the date of the article; and `<p>`, which is a paragraph tag to show the summary of the article. As nearly all items in an RSS feed are optional, we used the `python.get()` operator instead of using index notation (square brackets), meaning that if any information is missing, it'll simply be omitted from our final HTML rather than causing a runtime error.

For the sake of clarity, we didn't do any exception handling in this example; however, note that `feedparser` may well throw an exception on attempting to parse the BBC URL. If your local Internet connection is unavailable, the BBC server is down, or the provided feed is malformed, then `feedparser` will not be able to turn the feed into a Python dictionary. In a real application, we would add some exception handling and retry the logic here. In a real application, we'd also never build HTML within a Python string. We'll look at how to handle HTML properly in the next chapter. Fire up your web browser and take a look at the result. You should see a very basic page that looks similar to the following (although your news story will be different):

This is a great start, and we're now serving dynamic content (that is, content that changes automatically in response to user or external events) to our application's hypothetical users. However, ultimately, it's not much more useful than the static string. Who wants to see a single news story from a single publication that they have no control over?

To finish off this chapter, we'll look at how to show an article from different publications based on URL routing. That is, our user will be able to navigate to different URLs on our site and view an article from any of several publications. Before we do this, let's take a slightly more detailed look at how Flask handles URL routing.

URL routing in Flask

Do you remember that we briefly mentioned Python decorators in the previous chapter? They're represented by the funny `@app.route("/")` line we had above our main function, and they indicate to Flask which parts of our application should be triggered by which URLs. Our base URL, which is usually something similar to `site.com` but in our case is the IP address of our VPS, is omitted, and we will specify the rest of the URL (that is, the path) in the decorator. Earlier, we used a single slash, indicating that the function should be triggered whenever our base URL was visited with no path specified. Now, we will set up our application so that users can visit URLs such as `site.com/bbc` or `site.com/cnn` to choose which publication they want to see an article from.

The first thing we need to do is collect a few RSS URLs. At the time of writing, all of the following are valid:

- **CNN**: `http://rss.cnn.com/rss/edition.rss`
- **Fox News**: `http://feeds.foxnews.com/foxnews/latest`
- **IOL**: `http://www.iol.co.za/cmlink/1.640`

First, we will consider how we might achieve our goals using static routing. It's by no means the best solution, so we'll implement static routing for only two of our publications. Once we get this working, we'll consider how to use dynamic routing instead, which is a simpler and more generic solution to many problems.

Instead of declaring a global variable for each of our RSS feeds, we'll build a Python dictionary that encapsulates them all. We'll make our `get_news()` method generic and have our decorated methods call this with the relevant publication. Our modified code looks as follows:

```
import feedparser
from flask import Flask
```

```
app = Flask(__name__)

RSS_FEEDS = {'bbc': 'http://feeds.bbci.co.uk/news/rss.xml',
             'cnn': 'http://rss.cnn.com/rss/edition.rss',
             'fox': 'http://feeds.foxnews.com/foxnews/latest',
             'iol': 'http://www.iol.co.za/cmlink/1.640'}

@app.route("/")
@app.route("/bbc")
def bbc():
    return get_news('bbc')

@app.route("/cnn")
def cnn():
    return get_news('cnn')

def get_news(publication):
  feed = feedparser.parse(RSS_FEEDS[publication])
  first_article = feed['entries'][0]
  return """<html>
    <body>
        <h1>Headlines </h1>
        <b>{0}</b> </ br>
        <i>{1}</i> </ br>
        <p>{2}</p> </ br>
    </body>
</html>""".format(first_article.get("title"), first_article.
get("published"), first_article.get("summary"))


if __name__ == "__main__":
  app.run(port=5000, debug=True)
```

Common mistakes:

If you're copying or pasting functions and editing the `@app.route`
decorator, it's easy to forget to edit the function name. Although
the name of our functions is largely irrelevant as we don't call them
directly, we can't have different functions share the same name as the
latest definition will always override any previous ones.

We still return the BBC news feed by default, but if our user visits the CNN or BBC routes, we will explicitly take the top article from respective publication. Note that we can have more than one decorator per function so that our bbc() function gets triggered by a visit to our base URL or to the /bbc path. Also, note that the function name does not need to be the same as the path, but it is a common convention that we followed in the preceding example.

Following this, we can see the output for our application when the user visits the /cnn page. The headline displayed is now from the CNN feed.

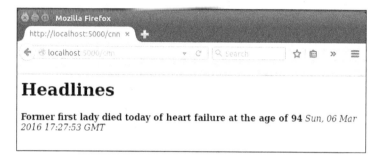

Now that we know how routing works in Flask, wouldn't it be nice if it could be even simpler? We don't want to define a new function for each of our feeds. What we need is for the function to dynamically grab the right URL based on the path. This is exactly what dynamic routing does.

In Flask, if we specify a part of our URL path in angle brackets < >, then it is taken as a variable and is passed to our application code. Therefore, we can go back to having a single get_news() function and pass in a <publication> variable, which can be used to make the selection from our dictionary. Any variables specified by the decorator must be accounted for in our function's definition. The first few lines of the updated get_news() function are shown as follows:

```
@app.route("/")
@app.route("/<publication>")
def get_news(publication="bbc"):
    # rest of code unchanged
```

In the code shown earlier, we added <publication> to the route definition. This creates an argument called publication, which we need to add as a parameter of the function directly below the route. Thus, we can keep our default value for the publication parameter as bbc, but if the user visits CNN, Flask will pass the cnn value as the publication argument instead.

The rest of the code remains unchanged, but it's important to delete the now unused bbc() and cnn() function definitions as we need the default route to activate our get_news() function instead.

It's easy to forget to *catch* the URL variables in the function definition. Any dynamic part of the route must contain a parameter of the same name in the function in order to use the value, so look out for this. Note that we gave our publication variable a default value of bbc so that we don't need to worry about it being undefined when the user visits our base URL. However, again, our code will throw an exception if the user visits any URL that we don't have as a key in our dictionary of feeds. In a real web application, we'd catch cases such as this and show an error to the user, but we'll leave error handling for later chapters.

Publishing our Headlines application

This is as far as we'll take our application in this chapter. Let's push the results to our server and configure Apache to display our headlines application instead of our Hello World application by default.

First, add your changes to the Git repository, commit them, and push them to the remote. You can do this by running the following commands (after opening a terminal and changing directory to the headlines directory):

```
git add headlines.py
git commit -m "dynamic routing"
git push origin master
```

Then, connect to the VPS with SSH and clone the new project there using the following commands:

```
ssh -i yourkey.pem root@123.456.789.123
cd /var/www
git clone https://<yourgitrepo>
```

Don't forget to install the new library that we now depend on. Forgetting to install dependencies on your server is a common error that can lead to a frustrating debugging. Keep this in mind. The following is the command for this:

```
pip install --user feedparser
```

Now, create the `.wsgi` file. I assume that you named your Git project `headlines` when creating the remote repository and that a directory named `headlines` was created in your `/var/www` directory when you did the preceding Git clone command. If you called your project something else and now have a directory with a different name, rename it to headlines (otherwise, you'll have to adapt a lot of the configuration we're about to do accordingly). To rename a directory in Linux, use the following command:

```
mv myflaskproject headlines
```

The command used earlier will rename the directory called `myflaskproject` to `headlines`, which will ensure that all the configuration to follow will work. Now, run the following:

```
cd headlines
```

```
nano headlines.wsgi
```

Then, insert the following:

```
import sys
sys.path.insert(0, "/var/www/headlines")
from headlines import app as application
```

Exit Nano by hitting the *Ctrl + X* key combo and enter *Y* when prompted to save changes.

Now, navigate to the `sites-available` directory in Apache and create the new `.conf` file using the following commands:

```
cd /etc/apache2/sites-available
```

```
nano headlines.conf
```

Next, enter the following:

```
<VirtualHost *>
    ServerName example.com

    WSGIScriptAlias / /var/www/headlines/headlines.wsgi
    WSGIDaemonProcess headlines
    <Directory /var/www/headlines>
       WSGIProcessGroup headlines
       WSGIApplicationGroup %{GLOBAL}
        Order deny,allow
        Allow from all
    </Directory>
</VirtualHost>
```

Save the file and quit nano. Now, disable our old site, enable the new one, and restart Apache by running the following commands:

```
sudo a2dissite hello.conf
sudo a2enssite headlines.conf
sudo service apache2 reload
```

Try and visit the IP address of your VPS from your local machine, and if all went as expected, you should see the news headline as before! If not, don't worry. It's easy to make a mistake in some piece of configuration. It's most likely that your `headlines.wsgi` or `headlines.conf` file has a small error. The easiest way to find this is by looking at the most recent errors in your Apache error log, which would have been triggered when you attempted to visit the site. View this again with the following command:

```
sudo tail -fn 20 /var/log/apache2/error.log
```

Summary

That's it for this chapter. The major takeaways of this chapter were taking a look at how routing, both static and dynamic, are handled in Flask. You also learned a fairly messy way of formatting data using HTML and returning this to the user.

In the next chapter, we'll take a look at cleaner ways to separate our HMTL code from our Python code using Jinja templates. We'll also have our app display more than a single news story.

3
Using Templates in Our Headlines Project

In the last chapter, we saw one way of combining static HTML with dynamic content for creating a web page. But it's messy, and we don't want to hack away at Python strings for building our web pages. Mixing HTML and Python is not ideal for a few reasons: for one, it means if we ever want to change static text, such as that which appears in our headings, we have to edit our Python files, which also involves reloading these files into Apache. If we hire frontend developers to work on HTML, we run the risk of them breaking the unfamiliar Python code by mistake, and it's far more difficult to structure any other frontend code such as JavaScript and CSS correctly. Ideally, we should aim for complete segregation between the frontend and backend components. We can achieve this to a large extent using Jinja, but as with most aspects of life, some compromise will be necessary.

By the end of this chapter, we'll have extended our application to display more than a single headline for the chosen publication. We'll display several articles for each publication, each one having a link to the original article, and our logic and view components will largely be separated. In this chapter, we'll cover the following topics:

- Introducing Jinja
- Basic use of Jinja templates
- Advanced use of Jinja templates

Introducing Jinja

Jinja is a Python template engine. It allows us to easily define dynamic blocks of HTML which are populated by Python. HTML templates are useful even for static websites which have multiple pages. Usually, there are some common elements, such as headers and footers, on every page. Although it is possible to maintain each page individually for static websites, this requires that a single change be made in multiple places if the change is made to a shared section. Flask was built on top of Jinja, so although it is possible to use Jinja without Flask, Jinja is still an inherent part of Flask, and Flask provides several methods to work directly with Jinja. Generally, Flask assumes nothing about the structure of your application except what you tell it, and prefers providing functionality through optional plugins. Jinja is somewhat of an exception to this. Flask gives you Jinja by default, and assumes that you store all your Jinja templates in a subdirectory of your application named `templates`.

Once we've created templates, we'll make calls from our Flask app to render these templates. Rendering involves parsing the Jinja code, inserting any dynamic data, and creating pure HTML to be returned to a user's browser. All of this is done behind the scenes though, so it can get a bit confusing as to what is being done where. We'll take things one step at a time.

Basic use of Jinja templates

The first step to using Jinja templates is creating a directory in our application to contain our template files, so navigate to your `headlines` directory, and create a directory called `templates`. Unlike the previous steps, this name is expected by other parts of the application and is case sensitive, so take care while creating it. At the most basic level, a Jinja template can just be an HTML file, and we'll use the `.html` extension for all our Jinja templates. Create a new file in the `templates` directory called `home.html`. This will be the page that our users see when visiting our application, and will contain all the HTML that we previously had in a Python string.

 We'll only be using Jinja to build HTML files in this book, but Jinja is flexible enough for use in generating any text-based format. Although we use the `.html` extension for our Jinja templates, the files themselves will not always be pure HTML.

For now, put the following static HTML code into this file. We'll look at how to pass dynamic data between Python and our templates in the next step.

```
<html>
    <head>
        <title>Headlines</title>
```

```
        </head>
        <body>
            <h1>Headlines</h1>
            <b>title</b><br />
            <i>published</i><br />
            <p>summary</p>
        </body>
    </html>
```

Now in our Python code, instead of building up the string and returning that in our routing function, we'll render this template and return it. In `headlines.py`, add an import at the top:

```
from flask import render_template
```

The `render_template` function is the magic which takes a Jinja template as input and produces pure HTML, capable of being read by any browser, as the output. For now, some of the magic is lost, as we'll give it pure HTML as input and view the same as output in our browser.

Rendering a basic template

In your `get_news()` function, remove the `return` statement, which contains our triple-quoted HTML string as well. Leave the previous lines which grab the data from `feedparser`, as we'll be using that again soon.

Update the `return` statement, so that the `get_news()` function now looks as follows:

```
@app.route("/")
@app.route("/<publication>"
def get_news(publication="bbc"):
  feed = feedparser.parse(RSS_FEEDS[publication])
  first_article = feed['entries'][0]
  return render_template("home.html")
```

Although our current HTML file is pure HTML and not yet using any of the Jinja syntax that we'll see later, we're actually already doing quite a bit of magic. This call looks in our `templates` directory for a file named `home.html`, reads this, parses any Jinja logic, and creates an HTML string to return to the user. Once you've made both the preceding changes, run your application again with `python headlines.py`, and navigate to `localhost:5000` in your browser.

Again, we've gone a step backwards in order to advance. If you run the app and view the result in your browser now, you should see something similar to our original page, except that instead of the real news data, you'll just see the strings **title**, **published**, and **summary** as seen in the following image:

Let's take a look at how to populate these fields inside our render_template call so that we can see real news content again.

Passing dynamic data to our template

First, in our Python file, we'll pass each of these as named variables. Update the get_news() function again, and pass all the data that you need to display to the user as arguments to render_template(), as follows:

```
@app.route("/")
@app.route("/<publication>"
def get_news(publication="bbc"):
    feed = feedparser.parse(RSS_FEEDS[publication])
    first_article = feed['entries'][0]
    render_template("home.html",
                    title=first_article.get("title"),
                    published=first_article.get("published"),
                    summary=first_article.get("summary"))
```

The render_template function takes the filename of the template as its first argument, and can then take an arbitrary number of named variables as subsequent arguments. The data in each of these variables will be available to the template, using the variable name.

Displaying dynamic data in our template

In our `home.html` file, we simply need to put two braces on either side of our placeholders. Change it to look like the following:

```
<html>
    <head>
        <title>Headlines</title>
    </head>
    <body>
        <h1>Headlines</h1>
        <b>{{title}}</b><br />
        <i>{{published}}</i><br />
        <p>{{summary}}</p>
    </body>
</html>
```

Double braces, {{ }}, indicate to Jinja that anything inside them should not be taken as literal HTML code. Because our *placeholders*, *title*, *published*, and *summary*, are the same as our Python variable names passed into the `render_template` call, just adding the surrounding braces means that the `render_template` call will substitute these for the real data, returning a pure HTML page. Try it out to make sure that we can see real news data again, as seen in the following image:

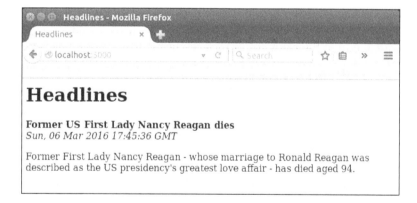

Advanced use of Jinja templates

Now we have perfect separation of our backend and frontend components, but our application doesn't do anything more than it did before. Let's take a look at how to display multiple news articles from a selected publication. We don't want to add three new arguments to our `render_template` call for each article (or dozens of additional arguments if we ever decide that we want to display more than just the title, date, and summary of an article).

Fortunately, Jinja can take over some of the logic from Python. This is where we have to be careful: we spent all that effort to separate our logic and view components, and when we discover how powerful the Jinja language actually is, it's tempting to move a lot of the logic into our template files. This would leave us back where we started with code that is difficult to maintain. However, in some cases it's necessary for our frontend code to handle some logic, such as now where we don't want to pollute our backend code with too many repeated arguments.

Using Jinja objects

The first thing to learn is how Jinja handles objects. All of the basic Python data structures, such as variables, objects, lists, and dictionaries, can be understood by Jinja and can be processed in a very similar way to what we are used to in Python. For example, instead of passing each of the three components of our article separately to our template, we could have passed in the `first_article` object and dealt with the separation in Jinja. Let's see how to do that. Change the Python code to pass in a single-named argument to `render_template`, that is `first_article`, and the frontend code to grab the bits we need from this.

The `render_template` call should now look like this:

```
render_template("home.html", article=first_article)
```

The template now has a reference called `article`, which we can use to get the same result as before. Change the relevant part of the home.html to read as follows:

```
<b>{{article.title}}</b><br />
<i>{{article.published</i><br />
<p>{{article.summary}}</p>
```

Note that accessing items from a dictionary is slightly different in Jinja as compared to Python. We use a full stop to access properties, so to access the title of the article, we use `{{article.title}}` as in the preceding example, instead of the Python equivalent `article["title"]` or `article.get("title")`. Our code is again neater, but yet again has no additional functionality.

Adding looping logic to our template

Without much extra effort, we can make the whole list of articles available to Jinja. In the Python code, change the `render_template` call to read as follows:

```
render_template("home.html", articles=feed['entries'])
```

You can remove the line directly above the preceding one in the code which defines the `first_article` variable, as we won't need it any more. Our template now has access to the full list of articles that we fetch through `feedparser`.

In our Jinja template, we could now add `{{articles}}` or `{{articles[0]}}` to see a full dump of all the information we're now passing, or just a dump of the first article respectively. You can try this as an intermediate step if you're curious, but in our next step we'll be looping through all the articles and displaying the information we want.

By giving our template more data to work with, we're passing along some of the logic responsibility that should ideally be handled by our Python code, but we can also deal with this very cleanly in Jinja. Similar to the way we use double braces, `{{ }}`, to indicate variables, we use the brace and percentage combination, `{% %}`, to indicate control logic. This will be clearer by looking at an example. Change the `<body>` part of the template code to read as follows:

```
<body>
    <h1>Headlines</h1>
    {% for article in articles %}
        <b>{{article.title}}</b><br />
        <i>{{article.published}}</i><br />
        <p>{{article.summary}}</p>
        <hr />
    {% endfor %}
</body>
```

We can see that the Jinja for loop is similar to Python. It loops through the *articles* list that we've passed in from the Python code, and creates a new variable, `article`, for each iteration of the loop, each time referring to the next item in the list. The `article` variable can then be used like any other Jinja variable (using the double braces). Because whitespace in Jinja is irrelevant, unlike Python, we must define where our loop ends with the `{% endfor %}` line. Finally, the `<hr />` in HTML creates a horizontal line which acts as a separator between each article.

Run the application locally with the new template file, and view the results in your browser. You should see something similar to the following image:

Adding hyperlinks to our template

Now we want to link each headline to the original article. Our user will probably find this useful—if a headline seems interesting, he or she can easily get to the full text of the article to read it. The owner of the RSS feed will also often require or request that anyone who uses the feed links back to the original articles. (Again, check for terms and conditions as published along with most big feeds.) Because we're passing the whole `article` object to our template already, we won't need to make any further changes to our Python code to achieve this; we simply need to make use of the extra data already available to us.

In the template file, search for the following:

```
<b>{{article.title}}</b><br />
```

Change this line to the following:

```
<b><a href="{{article.link}}">{{article.title}}</a></b><br />
```

If you're new to HTML, then there's quite a bit going on here. Let's pull it apart: the <a> tag in HTML indicates a hyperlink (usually displayed by default as blue and underlined in most browsers), the href attribute specifies the destination or URL of the link, and the link ends with the </a> tag. That is, any text between <a> and </a> will be clickable, and will be displayed differently by our user's browser. Note that we can use the double braces to indicate a variable even within the double quotation marks used to define the destination attribute.

If you refresh the page in your browser, you should now see the headlines as bold links, as in the following image, and clicking on one of the links should take you to the original article.

Pushing our code to the server

Now is a good time to push the code to our VPS. This is the last time we'll break down the steps of how to do this, but hopefully, you'd be familiar enough with Git and Apache by now that there won't be anything unexpected. On your local machine, from the headlines directory, run:

```
git add headlines.py
git add templates
git commit -m "with Jinja templates"
git push origin master
```

And on your VPS (SSH into it as usual), change to the appropriate directory, pull the updates from the Git repository, and restart Apache to reload the code:

```
cd /var/www/headlines
git pull
sudo service apache2 reload
```

Make sure everything has worked by visiting the IP address of your VPS from the web browser on your local machine and checking that you see the same output that we saw locally, as seen in the following image:

Summary

We now have a basic news summary site! You can display recent news from a number of different websites, see the headline, date, and summary for each recent article, and can click on any headline to visit the original article. You've only seen a tiny sample of the power of the Jinja language though—as we expand this project and other projects in future chapters, you'll see how it can be used for inheritance, conditional statements, and more.

In the next chapter, we'll add weather and currency information to our application, and look at ways to interact with our users.

4
User Input for Our Headlines Project

Remember how we allowed the user to specify the publication to be viewed by using `<variable>` parts in our URL? Although we were effectively getting input from our user, it's a way of retrieving input that has some pretty heavy limitations. Let's look at some more powerful ways to interact with our users, and add some more useful information to our application. We'll be making quite a few incremental changes to our code files from here on, so remember that you can always refer to the accompanying code bundle if you need an overview at any point.

In this chapter, we'll look at some more flexible and powerful ways to get input. We'll also bump into some more advanced Git features along the way, and take a moment to explain how to use them.

We'll cover the following topics in this chapter:

- Getting user input using HTTP GET
- Getting user input using HTTP POST
- Adding weather and currency data

Getting user input using HTTP GET

HTTP GET requests are the simplest way of retrieving input from the user. You might have noticed question marks in URLs while browsing the Web. When submitting a term in the search box on the website, your search term will usually appear in the URL, and look something like this:

```
example.com/search?query=weather
```

The bit after the question mark represents a named GET argument. The name is query and the value, weather. Although arguments like these are usually automatically created through HTML input boxes, the user can also manually insert them into the URL, or they can be part of a clickable link that is sent to the user. HTTP GET is designed to get limited, non-sensitive information from the user in order for the server to return a page as requested by the GET arguments. By convention, GET requests should never modify the server state in a way that produces side effects, that is, the user should be able to make exactly the same request multiple times and always be given exactly the same results.

GET requests are, therefore, ideal for allowing our user to specify which publication to view. Let's extend our Headlines project to incorporate selecting a headline based on a GET request. First, let's modify the Python code to do the following:

- Import the request context from Flask
- Remove the dynamic URL variable
- Check to see if the user has entered a valid publication as a GET argument
- Pass the user query and the publication to the template

Update the headlines.py file as follows:

```
import feedparser
from flask import Flask
from flask import render_template
from flask import request

app = Flask(__name__)

RSS_FEEDS = {'bbc': 'http://feeds.bbci.co.uk/news/rss.xml',
             'cnn': 'http://rss.cnn.com/rss/edition.rss',
             'fox': 'http://feeds.foxnews.com/foxnews/latest',
             'iol': 'http://www.iol.co.za/cmlink/1.640'}


@app.route("/")
def get_news():
        query = request.args.get("publication")
        if not query or query.lower() not in RSS_FEEDS:
                publication = "bbc"
        else:
                publication = query.lower()
        feed = feedparser.parse(RSS_FEEDS[publication])
        return render_template("home.html",
        articles=feed['entries']
```

```
if __name__ == "__main__":
    app.run(port=5000, debug=True)
```

The first new change is a new import for Flask's request context. This is another piece of Flask magic that makes our life easier. It provides a global context which our code can use to access information about the latest request made to our application. This is useful for us, because the GET arguments that our user passes along as part of a request are automatically available in `request.args`, from which we can access key-value pairs as we would with a Python dictionary (although it is immutable). The request context simplifies some other parts of request handling as well, which means that we don't have to worry about threads or the ordering of requests. You can read more about how the request context works, and what it does, at the following website:

```
http://flask-cn.readthedocs.org/en/latest/reqcontext/
```

We check to see if this has the publication key set by using the `get()` method, which returns `None`. if the key doesn't exist. If the argument is there, we make sure that the value is valid (that is, it is accounted for by our `RSS_FEEDS` mapping), and if it is, we return the matching publication.

We can test out the code by visiting our URL followed by the `get` argument, for example: `localhost:5000/?publication=bbc`. Unfortunately, from our user's experience, we've made the application less user-friendly, instead of more. Why did we do this? It turns out that our user doesn't have to modify the URL by hand—with a very small change, we can have the URL arguments populated automatically so that the user doesn't have to touch the URL at all. Modify the `home.html` template, and add the following HTML below the heading:

```html
<form>
    <input type="text" name="publication" placeholder="search" />
    <input type="submit" value="Submit" />
</form>
```

This is quite straightforward, but let's pick it apart to see how it all works. First we create an HTML form element. By default, this will create an HTTP GET request when submitted, by passing any inputs as GET arguments into the URL. We have a single text input which has the name `publication`. This name is important as the GET argument will use this. The `placeholder` is optional, but it will give our user a better experience as the browser will use it to indicate what the text field is intended for. Finally, we have another input of type `submit`. This automatically creates a nice **Submit** button for our form which, when pressed, will grab any text in the input and submit it to our Python backend.

Save the template, and reload the page to see how it works now. You should see the input form at the top of the page, as seen in the following screenshot. We've gained a lot of functionality for four lines of HTML, and now we can see that, although GET arguments initially looked like they were creating more mission and admin, they actually make our web application much simpler and more user-friendly.

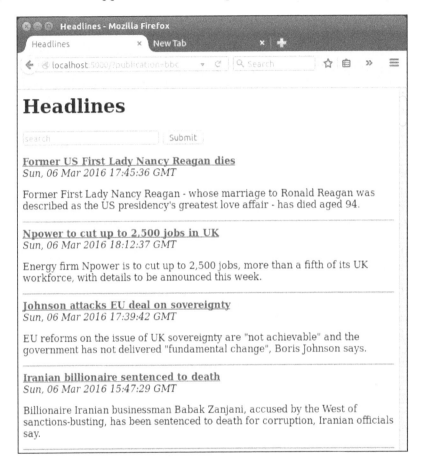

Getting user input using HTTP POST

The alternative to HTTP GET is HTTP POST, and it may not always be immediately obvious which one to use. HTTP POST is used to post larger chunks of data or more sensitive data to the server. Data sent through POST requests is not visible in the URL, and although this does not make it inherently more secure (it does not by default provide encryption or validation), it does offer some security advantages. URLs are often cached by the browser and suggested through autocomplete features next time the user types in a similar URL.

Data sent through GET requests may, therefore, be retained. Using POST also prevents someone from seeing the data by looking over the user's shoulder (shoulder surfing). Passwords especially are often obscured on input by using HTML password fields, making them appear as asterisks (********) or dots (•••••••) in the browser. The data would still be clearly visible in the URL if sent using GET however, and so POST should always be used instead.

Although our search query is hardly confidential or excessively long, we're going to take a moment now to see how we'd implement the same functionality using POST instead of GET. If you just want to get ahead with finishing off our Headlines application, feel free to skip this section, but keep in mind that we'll be using POST requests in later projects without extended explanation. Once we're done with the POST example, we'll revert our application to the state it is currently in (using the GET request), as this is much more suitable for our use case.

Creating a branch in Git

To make a change to our code base that we're not sure if we want, we'll use Git's branch functionality. Think of a branch as being like a fork in a road, except we can at any time change our mind and go back to the decision point. First, we need to make sure our current branch (master) is up to date—that all our local changes are committed. Open a terminal, and run the following commands from the headlines directory:

```
git add headlines.py
git add templates/home.html
git commit -m "Using GET"
git push origin master
```

We don't strictly need to push it to the server—Git keeps a full revision history locally, and our changes would still be theoretically safe without the push. However, our code is in a working state, so there's no harm making the backup to remote. Now we're going to create the new branch and switch to using it to make our next set of changes:

```
git branch post-requests
git checkout post-requests
```

We're now working in a new branch of our codebase. Usually, we'd eventually merge this branch back into our master branch, but in our case, we'll just abandon it once we're done with what we need. It's quite hard to visualize what's happening as Git does most things behind the scenes, so it's worth reading up about Git if you're interested, and are likely to use it for future projects. Otherwise, just think of this as a checkpoint so that we can freely experiment without the worry of messing up our code.

Adding POST routes in Flask

To use a POST request, we need to make some small changes to our Python and HTML code. In the `headlines.py` file, make the following changes:

- Change `request.args.get` to `request.form.get`
- Change `@app.route("/")` to `@app.route("/", methods=['GET', 'POST'])`

The reason for the first change is that we are now grabbing the user data from a form, so Flask automatically makes this available to us in `request.form`. This works the same way as `request.get` except that it gathers data from POST requests instead of from GETs. The second change is not quite as obvious. What we haven't mentioned before is that all route decorators can specify how the function can be accessed: either through GET requests, POST requests, or both. By default, only GET is permitted, but we now want our default page to be accessible by either GET (when we just visit the home main page and are given BBC as a default), or POST (for when we've requested the page through our form with the additional query data). The `methods` parameter accepts a list of HTTP methods which should be permitted to access that particular route of our application.

Making our HTML form use POST

Our template needs similar changes. Change the opening `<form>` tag in the `home.html` file to read:

```
<form action="/" method="POST">
```

Just as with Flask, HTML forms use GET by default, so we have to explicitly define that we want to use POST instead. The `action` attribute isn't strictly necessary, but usually, when we use POST, we redirect users to a confirmation page or similar, and the URL for the following page would appear here. In this case, we're explicitly saying that we want to be redirected to the same page after our form has been submitted.

Save the changes to the Python and HTML files, and refresh the page in your browser to see the changes take effect. The functionality should be exactly the same except that we don't see any data in the URL. This can be cleaner for many applications, but in our case, it is not what we want. For one, we'd like the search term to be cached by our users' browsers. If a user habitually makes a query for FOX, we want the browser to be able to autocomplete this after he begins typing in the URL for our application. Furthermore, we'd like our users to be able to easily share links that include the query.

If a user (let's call him Bob) sees a bunch of interesting headlines after typing **cnn** into our application, and wants to share all of these headlines with another user (Jane), we don't want Bob to have to message Jane, telling her to visit our site, and type a specific query into the search form. Instead, Bob should be able to share a URL that allows Jane to directly visit the page exactly as he saw it (for example, `example.com/?publication=cnn`). Jane can simply click on the link sent by Bob and view the same headlines (assuming she visits our page before the RSS feed is updated).

Reverting our Git repository

We need to revert the code to how we had it before. Because all the changes in the previous section were made in our experimental post-request branch, we don't need to manually re-edit the lines we changed. Instead, we'll commit our changes to this branch, and then switch back to our master branch, where we'll find everything as we left it. In your terminal, run the following:

```
git add headlines.py
git add templates/home.html
git commit -m "POST requests"
git checkout master
```

Open the `headlines.py` and `templates/home.html` files to be sure, but they should be exactly as we left them before experimenting with POST!

Adding weather and currency data

Now let's add some more functionality. We're showing media headlines from three different sources, but our user is probably interested in more than current affairs. We're going to see how easy it is to display the current weather and some exchange rates at the top of the page. For the weather data, we'll be using the OpenWeatherMap API, and for currency data, we'll be using Open Exchange Rates. At the time of writing, these APIs are freely available, although they both require registration.

Introducing the OpenWeatherMap API

In your web browser, visit the URL `http://api.openweathermap.org/data/2.5/weather?q=London,uk&units=metric&appid=cb932829eacb6a0e9ee4f38bfbf112ed`. You should see something that looks similar to the following screenshot:

This is the JSON weather data for London which is designed to be read automatically instead of by humans. Before looking at how to go about reading this data into our Headlines application, note that the URL we visited has an `appid` parameter. Even though the weather data is provided for free, every developer who accesses the data needs to sign up for a free account with OpenWeatherMap, and get a unique API key to pass as the value for the `appid` parameter. This is to prevent people from abusing the API by making too many requests, and hogging the available bandwidth. At the time of writing, OpenWeatherMap allows 60 calls to the API per minute and 50,000 per day as part of their free access plan, so it's unlikely that we'll be hitting these limits for our project.

Signing up with OpenWeatherMap

You should sign up for your own API key instead of using the one published in this book. Generally, your API key should remain a secret, and you should avoid sharing it (especially avoid publishing it in a book). To get your own API key, head over to `www.openweathermap.org` , and complete their sign-up progress by clicking the sign-up link at the top of the page. Fill out an e-mail address, username, and password. The registration page should look similar to the following screenshot:

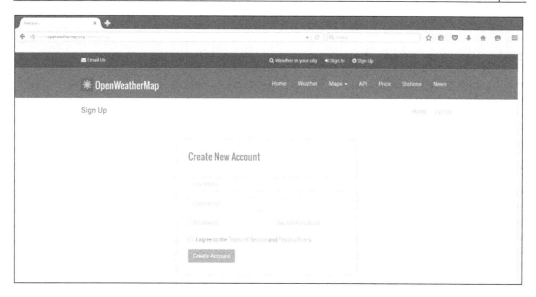

Retrieving your OpenWeatherMap API key

Once you've signed up, you'll be able to log into OpenWeatherMap. You can the find your personal API key by navigating to home.openweathermap.org and scrolling down to the **API key** text box. You should see your API key as indicated by the red rectangle in the following image:

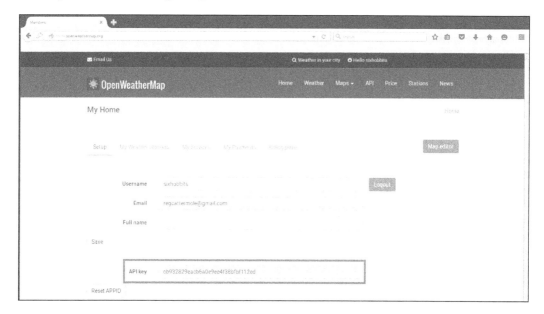

Copy the key to your clipboard, as we'll be using it in our Python code soon.

Parsing JSON with Python

Now we can access structured weather data over HTTP by using a URL. But doing so in our browser isn't much good, as we want to read this data automatically from our Python code. Luckily, Python has a bunch of useful standard libraries for exactly this use case!

Introducing JSON

JSON is a structured data format very similar to a Python dictionary, as should be apparent from the preceding sample. In fact, in this case it's identical, and we could very simply convert it to a Python dictionary to use in our Flask application by loading it as a string and running the built-in Python `eval` function on it. However, JSON is not always identical to a Python dictionary. For example, it uses `true` and `false` instead of `True` and `False` (note the case difference)—and passing anything that we don't have full control over to `eval()` is generally a bad idea. Therefore, we'll use the `Python json` library to safely parse it. We'll also use the Python `urllib2` library to download the data from the web, and the Python `urllib` library to correctly encode URL parameters.

Retrieving and parsing JSON in Python

For retrieving and parsing JSON in Python, the first step is to add the three new imports that we need to our `headlines.py` file:

```
import json
import urllib2
import urllib
```

Style tip:

> For good Python style, keep the imports ordered alphabetically. You can read more about the conventions for ordering imports at the following site: `https://www.python.org/dev/peps/pep-0008/#imports`

Now add a new function, `get_weather()`, which will make a call to the weather API with a specific query. It's pretty straightforward, and looks like the following code. Replace the `<your-api-key-here>` placeholder with the API key that you copied from the OpenWeatherMap page.

```
def get_weather(query):
    api_url = http://api.openweathermap.org/data/2.5/
    weather?q={}&units=metric&appid=<your-api-key-here>
```

```
query = urllib.quote(query)
url = api_url.format(query)
data = urllib2.urlopen(url).read()
parsed = json.loads(data)
weather = None
if parsed.get("weather"):
    weather = {"description":
                parsed["weather"][0]["description"],
              "temperature":parsed["main"]["temp"],
              "city":parsed["name"]
              }
return weather
```

We use the same URL we looked at earlier in our browser, but we make the query part-configurable so that the city for which we retrieve the weather data is dynamic. We use `urllib.quote()` on the query variable, as URLs cannot have spaces in them, but the names of the cities that we want to retrieve weather for may contain spaces. The `quote()` function handles this for us by, for example, translating a space to "%20", which is how spaces are represented in URLs. Then we load the data over HTTP into a Python string by using the `urllib2` library. As in our feedparsing example, downloading data over the Internet is always potentially unstable, and for a real-world application, we would need to add some exception handling, and retry logic here.

We then use the json library's `loads()` function (load string) to convert the JSON string that we downloaded into a Python dictionary. Finally, we manually build up a simpler Python dictionary based on the JSON one returned by the API, as OpenWeatherMap supplies a whole bunch of attributes that we don't need for our application.

Using our weather code

Now make two small changes to the `get_news()` function in order to use our `get_weather()` function. We need to call the `get_weather()` function (for now we'll just pass in London as a constant), and then pass the weather data to our template. The `get_news()` function should now look as follows:

```
@app.route("/")
def get_news():
    query = request.args.get("publication")
    if not query or query.lower() not in RSS_FEEDS:
        publication = "bbc"
    else:
        publication = query.lower()
    feed = feedparser.parse(RSS_FEEDS[publication])
    weather = get_weather("London,UK")
```

```
        return render_template("home.html",
        articles=feed["entries"],
        weather=weather)
```

This now loads the simplified data for London into the `weather` variable, and passes it along to our template file so that we can display the data to our users.

Displaying the weather data

Now we just need to adapt our template to account for the extra data. We'll display the weather data just above the news headlines, and add some level 2 headings to keep the different sections of our application organized.

Add the following three lines to the `home.html` template, right after the opening `<h1>` tag:

```
<body>
  <h1>Headlines</h1>
  <h2>Current weather</h2>
  <p>City: <b>{{weather.city}}</b></p>
  <p>{{weather.description}} |{{weather.temperature}}&#8451;</p>
  <h2>Headlines</h2>
```

There's nothing here that we haven't seen before. We simply grab the sections we want out of our weather variable using braces. The funny `&#8451;` part is to display the symbol for degrees Celsius. If you're one of those people who is able to make sense of the notion of Fahrenheit, then remove the `&units=metric` from the API URL (which will tell OpenWeatherData to give us the temperatures in Fahrenheit), and display the *F* symbol for our users by using `&#8457;` in your template instead.

Allowing the user to customize the city

As mentioned earlier, we would not always want to display the weather for London. Let's add a second search box for city! Searching is usually hard, because data input by users is never consistent, and computers love consistency. Luckily, the API that we're using does a really good job of being flexible, so we'll just pass on the user's input directly, and leave the difficult bit for others to deal with.

Adding another search box to our template

We'll add the search box to our template exactly as before. This form goes directly under the *Current weather* heading in the `home.html` file.

```
<form>
  <input type="text" name="city" placeholder="weather search">
```

```
    <input type="submit" value="Submit">
</form>
```

The form defined in the preceding code snippet simply uses a named text input and a submit button, just like the one we added for the publication input.

Using the user's city search in our Python code

In our Python code, we need to look for the `city` argument in the GET request. Our `get_news()` function is no longer well-named, as it does more than simply getting the news. Let's do a bit of refactoring. Afterwards, we'll have a `home()` function that makes calls to get the news and the weather data (and later on the currency data), and our `get_news()` function will again only be responsible for getting news. We're also going to have quite a few defaults for different things, so instead of hard-coding them all, we'll add a `DEFAULTS` dictionary as a global, and whenever our code can't find information in the GET arguments, it'll fall back to getting what it needs from there. The changed parts of our code (excluding the imports, global URLs, and the main section at the end) now look like this:

```python
# ...

DEFAULTS = {'publication':'bbc',
            'city': 'London,UK'}

@app.route("/")
def home():
    # get customized headlines, based on user input or default
    publication = request.args.get('publication')
    if not publication:
        publication = DEFAULTS['publication']
    articles = get_news(publication)
    # get customized weather based on user input or default
    city = request.args.get('city')
    if not city:
        city = DEFAULTS['city']
    weather = get_weather(city)
return render_template("home.html", articles=articles,
weather=weather)

def get_news(query):
    if not query or query.lower() not in RSS_FEEDS:
        publication = DEFAULTS["publication"]
    else:
        publication = query.lower()
    feed = feedparser.parse(RSS_FEEDS[publication])
```

```
        return feed['entries']
def get_weather(query):
    query = urllib.quote(query)
    url = WEATHER_URL.format(query)
    data = urllib2.urlopen(url).read()
    parsed = json.loads(data)
    weather = None
    if parsed.get('weather'):
        weather =
        {'description':parsed['weather'][0]['description'],
         'temperature':parsed['main']['temp'],
         'city':parsed['name']
        }
    return weather
```

Now we have a good separation of concerns—our get_weather() function gets weather data, our get_news() function gets news, and our home() function combines the two and handles the user's input to display customized data to our visitors.

Checking our new functionality

If all went well, we should now have a site that displays customizable news and weather data. The weather search, as mentioned, is pretty flexible. Give it a go with some different inputs—you should see a page similar to the following image:

Handling duplicate city names

The OpenWeatherMap API handles duplicate city names well, although the defaults are sometimes a bit counter-intuitive. For example, if we search for Birmingham, we'll get the one in the USA. If we want to look for the Birmingham in the UK, we can search for Birmingham, UK. In order to not confuse our viewers, we'll make a small modification for displaying the country next to the city. Then they'll immediately be able to see if they get results for a city different from what they were expecting. If you examine the full API response from our weather call, you'll find the country code listed under `sys` — we'll grab that, add it to our custom dictionary, and then display it in our template.

In the `get_weather` function, modify the line where we build the dictionary:

```
weather = {'description': parsed['weather'][0]['description'],
           'temperature': parsed['main']['temp'],
           'city': parsed['name'],
           'country': parsed['sys']['country']
          }
```

And in our template, modify the line where we display the city to read as follows:

```
<p>City: <b>{{weather.city}}, {{weather.country}}</b></p>
```

Check that its working – if you restart the application and reload the page, you should see that typing `Birmingham` into to the **Current weather** search box now displays the country code next to the city name.

Currency

Currency data is considered more valuable than weather data. Many commercial services offer APIs that are frequently updated and very reliable. However, the free ones are a bit rare. One service that offers a limited API for free is Open Exchange Rates—and again, we need to register a free account to get an API key.

Getting an API key for the Open Exchange Rates API

Head over to openexchangerates.com, and complete their registration process. After clicking on the **Sign up** link, it may look like they only have paid plans, as these are more prominently displayed. However, underneath the large paid plan options, there is a single line of text describing their free offering with a link to select it. Click on this, and enter your details.

If you are not automatically redirected, head over to your dashboard on their site, and you'll see your **API key** (App ID) displayed. Copy this, as we'll need to add it to our Python code. You can see an example of where to find your API key in the following screenshot:

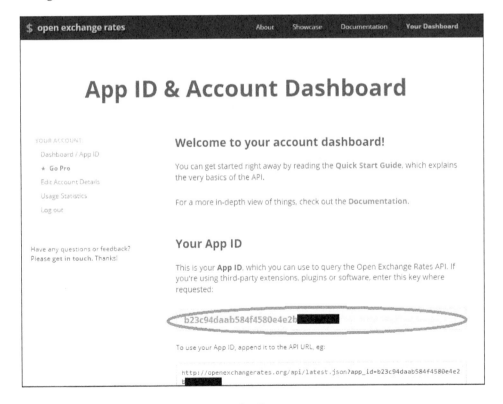

Using the Open Exchange Rates API

The `currency` API returns JSON just like the `weather` API, so we can integrate it into our Headlines application very easily. We need to add the URL as a global, and then add a new function to calculate rates. Unfortunately, the free version of the API is restricted to returning all the major currencies against the United States Dollar, so we will have to calculate our own approximate rates for conversions not involving the dollar, and rely on a perfect market to keep our information as accurate as possible (see `http://en.wikipedia.org/wiki/Triangular_arbitrage`).

Add the variable `CURRENCY_URL` to your globals below the existing `WEATHER_URL`, as seen in the following code snippet. You'll need to substitute your own App ID.

```
WEATHER_URL =
"http://api.openweathermap.org/data/2.5/weather?q={}
&units=metric&APPID=<your-api-key-here>"
CURRENCY_URL =
"https://openexchangerates.org//api/latest.json?
app_id=<your-api-key-here>"
```

Add the `get_rates()` function as follows:

```
def get_rate(frm, to):
        all_currency = urllib2.urlopen(CURRENCY_URL).read()

        parsed = json.loads(all_currency).get('rates')
        frm_rate = parsed.get(frm.upper())
        to_rate = parsed.get(to.upper())
        return to_rate/frm_rate
```

Note the calculation that we do at the end. If the request was from USD to any of the other currencies, we could simply grab the correct number from the returned JSON. But in this case, the calculation is simple enough, and it's therefore not worth adding the extra step of logic to work out if we need to do the calculation or not.

Using our currency function

Now we need to call the `get_rates()` function from our `home()` function, and pass the data through to our template. We also need to add default currencies to our `DEFAULTS` dictionary. Make the changes as indicated by the highlighted code that follows:

```
DEFAULTS = {'publication':'bbc',
            'city': 'London,UK',
            'currency_from':'GBP',
            'currency_to':'USD'
```

```
    }

@app.route("/")
def home():
    # get customized headlines, based on user input or default
    publication = request.args.get('publication')
    if not publication:
        publication = DEFAULTS['publication']
    articles = get_news(publication)
    # get customized weather based on user input or default
    city = request.args.get('city')
    if not city:
        city = DEFAULTS['city']
    weather = get_weather(city)
    # get customized currency based on user input or default
    currency_from = request.args.get("currency_from")
    if not currency_from:
        currency_from = DEFAULTS['currency_from']
    currency_to = request.args.get("currency_to")
    if not currency_to:
        currency_to = DEFAULTS['currency_to']
    rate = get_rate(currency_from, currency_to)
    return render_template("home.html", articles=articles,
    weather=weather,
                            currency_from=currency_from, currency_
to=currency_to, rate=rate)
```

Displaying the currency data in our template

Finally, we need to modify our template to display the new data. Underneath the
weather section in home.html, add:

```
<h2>Currency</h2>
1 {{currency_from}} = {{currency_to}} {{rate}}
```

As always, check that everything is working in your browser. You should see
the default currency data of the British Pound to US Dollar conversion as in the
following image:

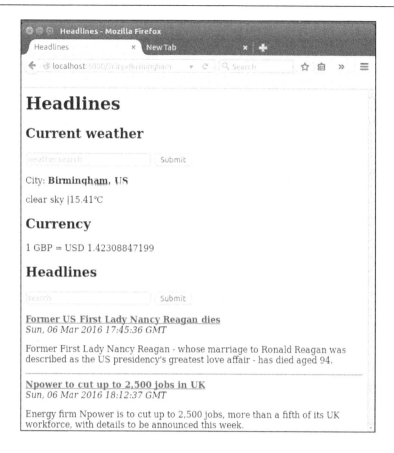

Adding inputs for the user to select currency

Now we need to add yet another user input to customize which currencies to display. We could easily add another text search like we did for the previous two, but this gets messy. We need two bits of input from the user: the *from* currency and the *to* currency. We could add two inputs, or we could ask the user to enter both into the same input, but the former makes our page pretty cluttered, and the latter means we need to worry about properly splitting the user input data (which is almost certainly not consistent). Instead, let's look at a different input element, the HTML select. You've almost certainly seen these on other web pages—they're drop-down menus with a list of values that the user can choose from. Let's see how to build them in HTML, and how to grab the data from them in Flask.

Creating an HTML select drop-down element

First, let's hard-code four currencies in each drop-down menu. The code should be inserted right below the **Currency** heading in the `home.html` template, and it looks like this:

```
<form>
    from: <select name="currency_from">
            <option value="USD">USD</option>
            <option value="GBP">GBP</option>
            <option value="EUR">EUR</option>
            <option value="ZAR">ZAR</option>
        </select>

    to: <select name="currency_to">
            <option value="USD">USD</option>
            <option value="GBP">GBP</option>
            <option value="EUR">EUR</option>
            <option value="ZAR">ZAR</option>
        </select>
        <input type="submit" value="Submit">
</form>
```

The name used for the GET request argument is an attribute of the select tag itself (similar to the name attribute used in our `<input type="text">` tags). In our case, these are `currency_from` and `currency_to`, which we specified in our Python code earlier. The value is slightly more tricky — we have the value that's passed in our GET request (for example, `currency_from=EUR`), and then the value that is displayed to the user. In this case, we'll use the same for both — the currency code — but this is not compulsory. For example, we could use the full name of the currency, such as United States Dollar, in the display value, and the code in the value that's passed in the request. The argument value is specified as an attribute of the option tags, each a child of `<select>`. The display value is inserted between the opening and closing `<option>` and `</option>` tags.

Test this out to make sure it's working, by saving the template and reloading the page. You should see drop-down inputs appear, as in the following image:

Adding all the currencies to the select input

Of course, we could do what we did in the preceding section for the full list. But we're programmers, not data capturers, so we'll make the list dynamic, insert the options using a `for` loop, and keep our template up-to-date and clean. To get the list of currencies, we can simply take the keys of our JSON `all_currency` object, in order to make our `get_rate()` function return a tuple—the calculated rate and the list of currencies. We can then pass the (sorted) list to our template, which can loop through them and use them to build the drop-down lists. The changes for this are shown as follows:

Make the following changes in the `home()` function:

```
if not currency_to:
    currency_to=DEFAULTS['currency_to']
rate, currencies = get_rate(currency_from, currency_to)
return render_template("home.html", articles=articles,
weather=weather,
currency_from=currency_from, currency_to=currency_to,
rate=rate,
currencies=sorted(currencies))
```

In the `get_rate()` function:

```
frm_rate = parsed.get(frm.upper())
to_rate = parsed.get(to.upper())
return (to_rate / frm_rate, parsed.keys())
```

And in the `home.html` template:

```
<h2>Currency</h2>
<form>
        from: <select name="currency_from">
              {% for currency in currencies %}
                  <optionvalue="{{currency}}">
                  {{currency}}</option>
              {% endfor %}
              </select>

        to: <select name="currency_to">
              {% for currency in currencies %}
                  <option value="{{currency}}">
                  {{currency}}</option>
              {% endfor %}

           </select>
        <input type="submit" value="Submit">
</form>
1 {{currency_from}} = {{currency_to}} {{rate}}
```

Displaying the selected currency in the drop-down input

After this, we should easily be able to see the exchange rate for any currency we want. One minor irritation is that the dropdowns always display the top item by default. It would be more intuitive for our users if they displayed the currently selected value instead. We can do this by setting the `selected="selected"` attribute in our select tag and a simple, one-line Jinja `if` statement to work out which line to modify. Change the `for` loops for the currency inputs in our `home.html` template to read as follows:

For the `currency_from` loop:

```
{% for currency in currencies %}
    <option value="{{currency}}"
    {{'selected="selected"' if currency_from==currency}}>
    {{currency}}</option>
{% endfor %}
```

For the `currency_to` loop:

```
{% for currency in currencies %}
    <option value="{{currency}}"
    {{'selected="selected"' if currency_to==currency}}>
    {{currency}}</option>
{% endfor %}
```

Reload the application and the page, and you should now be able to select any of the available currencies from both select inputs, and after the page has loaded with the desired currency data, the select inputs should automatically display the current currencies as well, as seen in the following image. After clicking on the select input, you should also be able to type on your keyboard and select the option based on the first letters of what you've typed.

We can now see news, weather, and currency data at the same time! You can refer to the complete code from the code bundle of the chapter.

Summary

In this chapter, we've looked at the difference between the HTTP GET and POST requests, and discussed where it's good to use which. Although we have no good use for HTTP POST at the moment, we will use it in future projects where we will be getting login data from our users. Luckily, the explanatory work we did with HTTP POST is not lost—we also took a look at some more advanced ways that Git can help us with version control, and our unused code is safely stored in a different branch of our code repository in case we need to refer back to it later. Last but not least, we added weather and currency data to our application, and looked at a few different options for allowing our user to input data into our application. We're nearly done with our first project!

In the next chapter, we'll do some cosmetic touch-ups, and look at remembering our users so that they don't have to carry out exactly the same actions every time they visit our site.

5
Improving the User Experience of Our Headlines Project

Wealthy business people who have to constantly make a good impression to keep up profitable relations sometimes employ personal assistants to study their acquaintances. The PA then stands behind the wealthy person at social events and whispers a few choice words to him or her about someone who is approaching to converse. The words have to be succinct but informative, such as "Paul Smith. One child, Jill. Recently travelled, Mauritius". Now, our business person can pretend that whoever has approached is a dear friend and talk all about his children and travels at some length without having the faintest clue of who the person actually is. This makes other people feel important and liked, and this can help our hypothetical millionaire become even richer.

Why is this relevant to web applications? Well, we want to do exactly the same thing. Users of our site who feel important and remembered are more likely to come back, so we need a digital PA to make the user feel as though we've taken the time and effort to remember who they are and what they like. We could build a database of our users to store what currency conversions they usually calculate and which cities' weather they are interested in and then display these to them by default. The issue with this strategy is that we'd need them to identify themselves with every visit, and most users would find the extra step of entering a username, and possibly a password, tedious and off-putting.

Enter HTTP cookies. These sly little things will lurk on our users' computers and act as digital PAs for us when our users make a second visit to our site, giving us information that we've acquired before but haven't bothered to remember. This sounds pretty underhand. At one point, the European Union thought this way and attempted to regulate the use of cookies, but they are everywhere and are simple and useful, and the regulation attempts were a bit underwhelming (take a look at `http://silktide.com/the-stupid-cookie-law-is-dead-at-last/`).

In their simplest form, cookies are simply key-value pairs that we store on our users' machines and ask their browser to automatically send back to us whenever they visit our site. The pros of this are that we don't have to keep and maintain a database and we don't have to explicitly ask users to tell us who they are. However, the cons are that we don't have control of the information and if a user changes computers, web browsers, or even just deletes our cookies, we'll no longer be able to identify him or her. Cookies are, therefore, perfect for an application such as the one we've built; it's not the end of the world if a user has to click a few times to get back to the media, currency, and weather information he or she searched for the last time, but it's nice if we can remember previous choices and display these automatically.

While we're on the topic of user experience (or UX as it's often referred to), our site looks as though it was made in the 1980s. We'll have a stronger focus on aesthetics in later chapters, but for now we'll also take a look at how to add some basic layout and colors to our site. As we're focusing on functionality and simplicity, it'll still be far from "modern-looking", but we'll add some building blocks to our toolkit that we'll use more carefully later on. We'll use **Cascading Style Sheets** (normally just called **CSS**) to achieve this. CSS is a great tool to enable a further separation of concerns; we have already mainly separated our logic (that is, our Python script) from our content (that is, our HTML templates). Now, we'll take a look at how CSS can help us separate our formatting (that is, the color, font, layout, and so on) from the rest of our content, such as the static text in our template files.

Now that we've had an overview of cookies and CSS, we'll get to looking at implementing them in Flask. This is the final chapter of our first project, and by the end of it, we'll have a Headlines application that includes cookies and CSS.

In this chapter, we'll look at the following topics:

- Adding cookies to our Headlines application
- Adding CSS to our Headlines application

Adding cookies to our Headlines application

Our application, at this point, has a couple of issues. Let's imagine a user, Bob, who lives in Seattle. Bob visits our site and sees the defaults for BBC, London, and conversion of GBP to USD. Bob wants to see the weather for Seattle, so he types `Seattle` into the **Weather search** bar and hits Enter. He glances at the returned weather and feels pretty depressed that it's cold and raining as usual, so he looks away from the weather further down the page and sees the BBC headlines. He would prefer CNN headlines, so he selects this publication from the drop-down menu and hits **Submit**. He reads through a couple of headlines before realizing that current affairs are even duller and more depressing than the weather. So, his eyes move back to the top of the page again to cheer himself up. He's confused; since changing his publication preference, the weather has defaulted back to London, where the weather is even worse! He closes our application and doesn't come back. If he were to come back, everything would display the defaults again.

The two immediate problems are:

- Not remembering our users' choices even while they stay on our site
- Not remembering our users' choices after they close our site and revisit at a later stage

Let's fix both of these issues.

Using cookies with Flask

Cookies, as introduced earlier, can be thought of as key-value pairs that we may or may not receive by default from return visitors. We need to change our app so that when a user makes choices, we create or update their cookie to reflect these changes, and when a user requests our site, we check to see whether a cookie exists and read as much of the unspecified information from this as possible. First, we'll look at how to set cookies and have our user's browser automatically remember information, and then we'll look at retrieving the information that we previously used cookies to store.

Setting cookies in Flask

Flask makes dealing with cookies as easy as ever. First, we need a couple more imports; we'll use the `datetime` library from Python to set the lifespan of our soon-to-exist cookies, and we'll use Flask's `make_response()` function to create a response object that we can set cookies on. Add the following two lines to your imports section in the `headlines.py` file:

```
import datetime
from flask import make_response
```

Earlier, we were simply rendering our template with the custom arguments and then returning it to our users' web browsers. In order to set cookies, we need an extra step. First, we'll create a response object with our new `make_response()` function and then set our cookie using this object. Finally, we'll return the entire response, which includes the rendered template and the cookies.

Substitute the last line of our `home()` function in `headlines.py` with the following lines:

```
response = make_response(render_template("home.html",
  articles=articles,
  weather=weather,
  currency_from=currency_from,
  currency_to=currency_to,
  rate=rate,
  currencies=sorted(currencies)))
expires = datetime.datetime.now() + datetime.timedelta(days=365)
response.set_cookie("publication", publication, expires=expires)
response.set_cookie("city", city, expires=expires)
response.set_cookie("currency_from",
  currency_from, expires=expires)
response.set_cookie("currency_to", currency_to, expires=expires)
return response
```

This is quite a big change from the simple return statement we had, so let's break it down a bit. First, we will wrap a `make_response()` call around our `render_template()` call instead of returning the rendered template directly. This means that our Jinja templates will be rendered, and all the placeholders will be replaced with the correct values, but instead of returning this response directly to our users, we will load it into a variable so that we can make some more additions to it. Once we have this response object, we will create a `datetime` object with a value of 365 days from today's date. Then, we will do a series of `set_cookie()` calls on our `response` object, saving all the user's selections (or refreshing the previous defaults) and setting the expiry time to a year from the time the cookie was set using our `datetime` object.

Finally, we will return our `response` object, which contains the HTML for the rendered template, and our four cookie values. On loading the page, our user's browser will save the four cookies, and we'll be able to retrieve the values if the same user visits our application again.

Retrieving cookies in Flask

Remembering the information is not much good if we don't do anything with it. We now set cookies as the final step before we send a response to our users. However, we need to check for the saved cookies when a user sends us a request. If you remember how we got named arguments from Flask's request object, you could probably guess how to get saved cookies. The following line will get the cookie named `publication` if it exists:

```
request.cookies.get("publication")
```

This is simple, right? The only tricky part is getting our fallback logic correct. We still want explicit requests to take the highest priority; that is, if a user enters text or selects a value from a drop-down menu, this will be what he or she wants irrespective of what we expect from previous visits. If there is no explicit request, we will look in the cookies to check whether we can grab a default from there. Finally, if we still have nothing, we will use our hardcoded defaults.

Writing the fallback logic to check for cookies

Let's just implement this logic for `publication` first. Add a new `if` block to our publication logic in the `home()` function of `headlines.py` to make it match the following:

```
# get customised headlines, based on user input or default
publication = request.args.get("publication")
if not publication:
    publication = request.cookies.get("publication")
    if not publication:
        publication = DEFAULTS["publication"]
```

Now, we will look in the GET arguments, fall back if necessary on the saved cookies, and finally fall back on our default value. Let's take a look at this working. Open your web browser and navigate to `localhost:5000`. Search for `Fox` in the **Publication** search bar and wait for the page to reload with Fox News headlines. Now, close your browser, reopen it, and load `localhost:5000` again. This time, you should see the Fox headlines without having to search for them, as in the following screenshot.

Note that there is no `publication` argument in the URL, and yet the headlines themselves are now from Fox News.

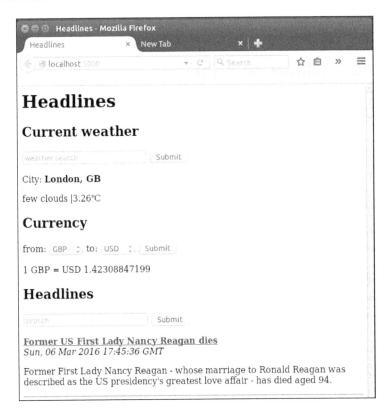

Retrieving the cookies for other data

We have basic cookies working for our publication, but we still want to read the cookies we potentially saved for weather and currency options. We could simply add the same if statement to each section of our code, substituting `city`, `currency_from`, and `currency_to` for `publication` as relevant, but making the same changes in many parts of our code is a strong sign that we need to do some refactoring.

Let's create a `get_value_with_fallback()` function instead that implements our fallback logic on a more abstract level. Add the new function to the `headlines.py` file and call it from the `home()` function, as shown here:

```
def get_value_with_fallback(key):
    if request.args.get(key):
        return request.args.get(key)
    if request.cookies.get(key):
        return request.cookies.get(key)
```

```
    return DEFAULTS[key]

@app.route("/")
def home():
    # get customised headlines, based on user input or default
    publication = get_value_with_fallback("publication")
    articles = get_news(publication)

    # get customised weather based on user input or default
    city = get_value_with_fallback("city")
    weather = get_weather (city)

    # get customised currency based on user input or default
    currency_from = get_value_with_fallback("currency_from")
    currency_to = get_value_with_fallback("currency_to")
    rate, currencies = get_rate(currency_from, currency_to)

    # save cookies and return template
    response = make_response(render_template("home.html",
      articles=articles,
      weather=weather, currency_from=currency_from,
      currency_to=currency_to, rate=rate,
      currencies=sorted(currencies)))
    expires = datetime.datetime.now() +
      datetime.timedelta(days=365)
    response.set_cookie("publication", publication,
      expires=expires)
    response.set_cookie("city", city, expires=expires)
    response.set_cookie("currency_from",
      currency_from, expires=expires)
    response.set_cookie("currency_to",
      currency_to, expires=expires)
    return response
```

Now, we should be able to submit the forms in any order and have all our options remembered as we would expect. Also, whenever we visit our site, it will automatically be configured with our most recently used options. Give it a go! You should be able to search for currency, weather, and headlines; then, close your browser; and revisit the site. The inputs you used most recently should appear by default.

In the following screenshot, we can see that no arguments are passed in the URL, and yet we are displaying weather data for Port Elizabeth in South Africa; currency data from the **Chinese Yuan (CNY)** to **Saint Helena Pound (SHP)**; and headlines from Fox News.

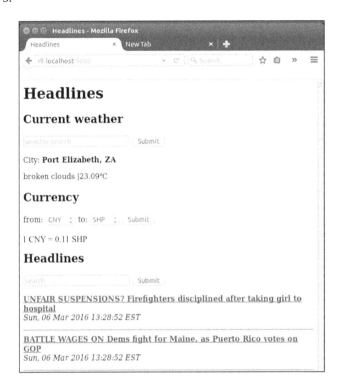

Adding CSS to our Headlines application

Our site remains pretty bare. There's a lot of white and some black. Most users prefer color, animations, borders, margins, and so on. As mentioned before, we're not really going to focus on aesthetics now, but we'll add some basic colors and styles.

External, internal, and inline CSS

There are a few ways that CSS can be added to a web page. The best way is to keep it completely separate from the HTML and save it in an external file, which is included in the HTML in a <link> element. This is sometimes referred to as the *external CSS*. The worst way is called *inline CSS*. Using the inline method, CSS is defined on a per element basis; this is considered bad practice as any changes to style require trawling through HTML to find the relevant sections.

Furthermore, many elements on a page often have the same or at least related styles to maintain color schemes and styles throughout the site. Using inline styles, therefore, often leads to a lot of code repetition, which we know to avoid.

For this project, we'll take a middle ground. We'll keep our CSS defined in our .html template files, but we'll define it all in a single place. This is because we haven't yet looked at how Flask handles files by convention, so keeping all our code in one place is simpler for now.

Adding our first CSS

CSS is quite straightforward; we will describe elements of our page by type, ID, class, and so on and define a number of properties for these, such as color, layout, padding, fonts, and so on. CSS is designed to *cascade*, that is, if we don't specify for a more specific element, it'll automatically inherit properties defined for a more general element. We'll go through the CSS itself fairly quickly, so if you've never heard of it before and would like to know more about it, now is the opportune moment to take a break and go through some CSS-specific resources. There are a lot of them online that a quick search will reveal; if you enjoyed the W3Schools HTML tutorial we mentioned earlier, you can find a similar CSS one here at http://www.w3schools.com/css/. Alternatively, dive in the deep end with the examples and brief explanations that follow!

First, let's add a better header to our site. We'll add a tagline beneath our top level heading, and surround it with a new <div> tag so that we can modify the entire header in the upcoming CSS. Modify the start of the home.html template to look as follows:

```
<div id="header">
    <h1>Headlines</h1>
    <p>Headlines. Currency. Weather.</p>
    <hr />
</div>
```

The <div> tag doesn't do anything by itself, and you can think of it as a container. We can use it to group logically related elements into the same element, which is very useful for CSS as we can then style all of the elements in a <div> tag at once.

CSS should be added into the <head> section of our template inside a <style> tag. Underneath the <title> tag in our home.html template, add the following code:

```
<style>
html {
    font-family: "Helvetica";
    background: white;
```

```
    }

    body {
        background: lightgrey;
        max-width: 900px;
        margin: 0 auto;
    }

    #header {
        background: lightsteelblue;
    }
    </style>
```

We defined the styles explicitly for three elements: the outer `<html>` element, the `<body>` element, and any element with an `id="header"` attribute. As all of our elements are within our `<html>` element, the font cascades automatically down everywhere (although it could still be overwritten explicitly by subelements). We set everything in our body element (which contains all the visible items of the page) to have a maximum width of 900 pixels. The `margin: 0 auto;` line means that there will be no margin at the top and bottom of the body, and an automatic margin on the left- and right-hand sides. This has the effect of centering everything on the page. The `background: white;` and `background: lightgrey;` lines mean that we'll have a centered main element with a light grey background inside the larger window, which is white. Finally, our defined header `div` will have a lightsteelblue background. Save the page with the added styles and refresh to see the effect. It should look similar to the following image:

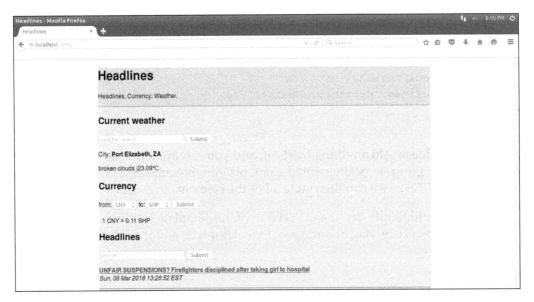

Let's take a look at how we can improve the aesthetics in the next section.

Browsers and caching

> Browsers often cache content that doesn't change often locally in order to display pages more quickly the next time you visit them. This is not ideal for development as you want to see the changes as you make them. If your styles don't seem to be doing what you'd expect, clear your browser's cache and try again. This can be done on most browsers by pressing *Ctrl + Shift + ESC* and selecting the relevant options from the menu that pops up.

Adding padding to our CSS

This is slightly more interesting than black on white, but it's still pretty ugly. One problem is that the text is right up against the margin of the color without any breathing room. We can fix this using *CSS padding*, which moves everything over from the top, right, bottom, left, or any combination by specified amounts.

We could add padding directly to our `<body>` tag as we want a nice left-hand side buffer for all the text. If you try this, you'll see the immediate issue; the padding will affect everything, including our `<div>` header and the `<hr>` tag that separates it from the rest of our content, which means that there will be a weird stripe of grey that isn't what we want. We'll fix the issue in a way that you'll soon use for nearly everything CSS-related—just add more divs! We need a *main* `<div>` header around all our subheadings and an inner header div so that we can pad the text in our header without padding the background color or the separator.

Adding more styles to our CSS

Add the following sections to your CSS to define left-hand side padding for our main and inner header divs and update the `#header` section to include some top padding:

```
#header {
  padding-top: 5;
  background: lightsteelblue;
}
#inner-header {
  padding-left: 10;
}
#main{
  padding-left: 10;
}
```

Adding the div tags to the template file

Now, let's add the divs themselves; the template code in `home.html` should be updated to look as follows:

```
<body>
    <div id="header">
        <div id="inner-header">
            <h1>Headlines</h1>
            <p>Headlines. Currency. Weather.</p>
        </div>
        <hr />
    </div>
    <div id="main">
        <h2>Current weather</h2>

... [ rest of the content code here ] ...

        {% endfor %}
    </div>
</body>
```

Styling our inputs

This makes the layout a bit more pleasant to look at because the text doesn't look like it's trying to sneak off the edge. The next major pain point is our input elements, which are very boring. Let's add some style to them as well. At the bottom of the CSS we have so far, add the following text:

```
input[type="text"], select {
    color: grey;
    border: 1px solid lightsteelblue;
    height: 30px;
    line-height:15px;
    margin: 2px 6px 16px 0px;
}
input[type="submit"] {
    padding: 5px 10px 5px 10px;
    color: black;
    background: lightsteelblue;
    border: none;
    box-shadow: 1px 1px 1px #4C6E91;
}
input[type="submit"]:hover{
    background: steelblue;
}
```

The first section styles our text input and select (that is, drop-down) elements. The text color is grey, it has a border that is of the same color as our heading, and we will make them a little bit bigger than the default ones we had before using height and line height. We also need to adjust the margins to make the text fit in the new size more naturally (if you're curious, leave out the margin line at the bottom of the first section and look at the result.) The second and third sections are to style our **Submit** buttons; one to define how they usually look and the other to define how they look when the mouse moves over them. Again, save these changes and refresh the page to see how they look. You should see something similar to the following screenshot:

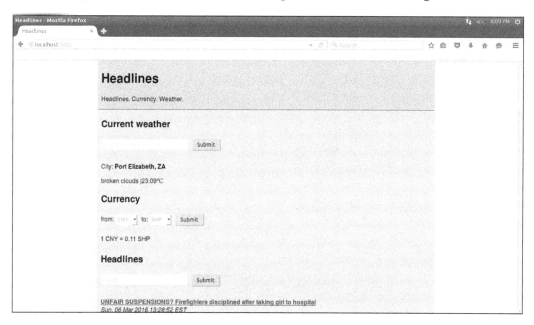

The final result will still not win any design awards, but at least you've learned the basics of CSS. One of the most frustrating parts of designing web pages is that each browser interprets CSS slightly differently (or in some cases, very differently). Cross-browser testing and validation is every web developer's arch nemesis, and in later chapters, we'll look at some tools and frameworks that can be used to mitigate the issues that arise from this potential lack of consistency.

Summary

We've made our site a bit more user-friendly in this chapter, both in terms of functionality (by remembering our users' choices through cookies) and aesthetics (using CSS). We'll come back to both of these topics in later projects, in which we'll use cookies to allow users to log in and some more advanced CSS. This is the end of our Headlines project; we have a functioning Headlines application that displays news, weather, and currency information.

In the next chapter, we'll start building a new project: an interactive crime map.

6
Building an Interactive
Crime Map

Our first project notably lacked any sort of long term memory. Although we worked around the issues using cookies to simulate long-term storage, we also saw the limitations of these. In this project, we'll build an interactive crime map that allows users to tag locations with details of witnessed or experienced criminal activities. As we want to keep the data for the long term and make it available to many users, we cannot rely on our users' local and temporary storage.

Therefore, the first step to our project will be setting up a MySQL database on our VPS and linking this to a new Flask web application. We'll use the Google Maps API to allow users to view our map and add new markers to it (in which each marker represents a crime).

We'll also have some more advanced user input than in our previous project, allowing users to filter their view of the map and add fairly complex data to the map. Therefore, we'll have a stronger focus on input validation and sanitization.

Our goal for the project is a web page containing an interactive map. The user should be able to submit new crimes by choosing a location for the map and entering a date, category, and description of the crime. The user should also be able to view all the previously recorded crimes as icons on the map and more details about any specific crime by selecting the relevant icon from the map. The point of the map is to be able to easily view areas with high crime rates as well as to assist investigators in detecting patterns and trends in crime.

A substantial chunk of this chapter is devoted to setting up a MySQL database on our VPS and creating a database for the crime data. This will be followed by us setting up a basic page containing a map and text box. We'll see how to link Flask to MySQL by storing data entered into the text box in our database.

As in the previous project, we'll avoid the frameworks and automation tools that we'd almost certainly use in a "real-world" project. As we will focus on learning, a lower level of abstraction is useful. Therefore, we won't be using **Object-relational Mapping (ORM)** for our database queries or a JavaScript framework for user input and interaction. This means that there will be some laborious writing of SQL and vanilla JavaScript, but it's important to fully understand why the tools and frameworks exist and what problems they solve, before diving in and using them blindly.

In this chapter, we'll cover:

- Setting up a new Git repository
- Understanding relational databases
- Installing and configuring MySQL on our VPS
- Creating our Crime Map database in MySQL
- Creating a basic database web application

Setting up a new Git repository

We'll create a new Git repository for our new code base as, although some of the setup will be similar, our new project should be completely unrelated to our first one. If you need more help with this step, head back to *Chapter 1*, *Hello, World!*, and follow the detailed instructions in the *Installing and using Git* section. If you feel confident, check whether you can do this just with the following summary:

- Head over to the website for Bitbucket, GitHub, or whichever hosting platform you used for the first project. Log in and create a new repository
- Name your repository `crimemap` and take note of the URL you're given
- On your local machine, fire up a terminal and run the following commands:
  ```
  mkdir crimemap
  cd crimemap
  git init
  git remote add origin <git repository URL>
  ```

We'll leave this repository empty for now as we need to set up a database on our VPS. Once we have the database installed, we'll come back here to set up our Flask project.

Understanding relational databases

In its simplest form, a relational database management system, such as MySQL, is a glorified spreadsheet program, such as Microsoft Excel. We use it to store data in rows and columns. Every row is a "*thing*" and every column is a specific piece of information about the "*thing*" in the relevant row. I put "*thing*" in inverted commas because we're not limited to storing objects. In fact, the most common example of a thing, both in the real world and in explaining databases, is data about people. A basic database storing information about customers of an e-commerce website could look something similar to the following:

ID	First name	Surname	E-mail address	Telephone
1	Frodo	Baggins	`fbaggins@example.com`	+1 111 111 1111
2	Bilbo	Baggins	`bbaggins@example.com`	+1 111 111 1010
3	Samwise	Gamgee	`sgamgee@example.com`	+1 111 111 1001

If we look from the left to the right in a single row, we will get all the information about one person. If we look in a single column from the top to the bottom, we will get one piece of information (for example, an e-mail address) for everyone. Both can be useful; if we want to add a new person or contact a specific person, we will probably be interested in a specific row. If we want to send a newsletter to all our customers, we will just be interested in the e-mail column.

So, why can't we just use spreadsheets instead of databases then? Well, if we take the example of an e-commerce store further, we will quickly see the limitations. If we want to store a list of all the items we have on offer, we can create another table similar to the preceding with columns such as `Item name`, `Description`, `Price`, and `Quantity in stock`. Our model continues to be useful; however, now, if we want to store a list of all the items Frodo has ever purchased, there's no good place to put the data. We could add 1,000 columns to our customer table (as seen earlier), such as `Purchase 1`, `Purchase 2`, and so on until `Purchase 1000`, and hope that Frodo never buys more than 1,000 items. This is neither scalable nor easy to work with. How do we get the description for the item Frodo purchased last Tuesday? Do we just store the `name` item in our new column? What happens with items that don't have unique names?

Soon, we will realize that we need to think about it backwards. Instead of storing the items purchased by a person in the `Customers` table, we need to create a new table called `Orders`, and store a reference to the customer in every order. Thus, an order "knows" which customer it belongs to, but a customer has no inherent knowledge of which orders belong to him/her.

While our model still fits into a spreadsheet at a push, as we grow our data model and size, our spreadsheet becomes more cumbersome. We need to do complicated queries, such as "I want to see all items that are in stock, have been ordered at least once in the last six months, and cost more than $10".

Enter **Relational Database Management Systems (RDBMS)**. They've been around for decades and are a tried-and-tested way of solving a common problem (such as storing data with complicated relations in an organized and accessible manner). We won't touch on their full capabilities in our Crime Map (in fact, we could probably store our data in a text file if we needed to), but if you're interested in building web applications, you will need a database at some point. So, let's start small and add the powerful MySQL tool to our growing toolbox.

I highly recommend that you learn more about databases! If the you experience in building our current project takes your fancy, go read and learn about databases. The history of RDBMS is interesting, and the complexities and subtleties of normalization and database varieties (including NoSQL databases, which we'll see some of in our next project) deserve more study time than we can devote to them in a book that focuses on Python web development.

Installing and configuring MySQL on our VPS

Installing and configuring MySQL is an extremely common task. You can, therefore, find it in prebuilt images or in scripts that build entire *stacks* for you. A common stack is called the **LAMP stack**, which stands for **Linux**, **Apache**, **MySQL**, and **PHP**, and many VPS providers provide a one-click LAMP stack image.

As we will use Linux and have already installed Apache manually, after installing MySQL, we'll be very close to the traditional LAMP stack; we will just use the P for Python instead of PHP. In keeping with our goal of "education first", we'll install MySQL manually, and configure it through the command line instead of installing a GUI control panel. If you've used MySQL before, feel free to set it up as you see fit.

MySQL and Git

 Keep in mind that neither our setup of MySQL nor the data we store in it is part of our Git repository. Be careful as any mistakes made at a database level, including misconfiguration or deleting data, will be harder to undo.

Installing MySQL on our VPS

Installing MySQL on our server is quite straightforward. SSH into your VPS and run the following commands:

```
sudo apt-get update
sudo apt-get install mysql-server
```

You should see an interface prompting you for a root password for MySQL. Enter a password and repeat it where prompted. Once the installation is complete, you can get a live SQL shell by typing the following:

```
mysql -p
```

Then, enter the password you chose earlier when prompted. We could create a database and schema using this shell, but we'd rather do this through Python; so, type quit and hit the *Enter* key to terminate the MySQL shell if you opened it.

Installing Python drivers for MySQL

As we want to use Python to talk to our database, we need to install another package. There are two main MySQL connectors for Python: *PyMySQL* and *MySQLdb*. The first is preferable from a simplicity and ease-of-use point of view. It is a pure Python library, which means that it has no dependencies. MySQLdb is a C extension and therefore has some dependencies, but it is a bit faster in theory. They work very similarly once installed. We'll use PyMySQL in our examples throughout this chapter.

To install it, run (while still on your VPS) the following command:

```
pip install --user pymysql
```

Creating our Crime Map database in MySQL

Some knowledge of SQL's syntax will be useful for the rest of this chapter, but you should be able to follow either way. The first thing we need to do is create a database for our web application. If you're comfortable using a command-line editor, you can create the following scripts directly on the VPS as this can make them easier to debug and we won't run them locally. However, developing over an SSH session is far from ideal; so, I recommend that you write them locally and use Git to transfer them to the server before running.

This may make debugging a bit frustrating, so be extra careful in writing these scripts. If you want, you can get them directly from the code bundle that comes with this book. In this case, you simply need to populate the user and password fields in the dbconfig.py file. correctly, and everything should work.

Creating a database setup script

In the crimemap directory in which we initialized our Git repository at the beginning of the chapter, create a python file called db_setup.py containing the following code:

```
import pymysql
import dbconfig
connection = pymysql.connect(host='localhost',
                             user=dbconfig.db_user,
                             passwd=dbconfig.db_password)

try:
        with connection.cursor() as cursor:
                sql = "CREATE DATABASE IF NOT EXISTS crimemap"
                cursor.execute(sql)
                sql = """CREATE TABLE IF NOT EXISTS crimemap.crimes (
id int NOT NULL AUTO_INCREMENT,
latitude FLOAT(10,6),
longitude FLOAT(10,6),
date DATETIME,
category VARCHAR(50),
description VARCHAR(1000),
updated_at TIMESTAMP,
PRIMARY KEY (id)
)"""
                cursor.execute(sql);
        connection.commit()
finally:
        connection.close()
```

Let's take a look at what this code does. First, we imported the PyMySQL library we just installed. We also imported dbconfig, which we'll create locally in a bit and populate with the database credentials (we don't want to store these in our repository). Then, we will create a connection to our database using localhost (because our database is installed on the same machine as our code) and the credentials that don't exist yet.

Now that we have connection to our database, we can get a cursor. You can think of a cursor a bit like the blinking object in your word processor that indicates where text will appear when you start typing. A database cursor is an object that points to a place in the database where we want to create, read, update, or delete data. Once we start dealing with database operations, there are various exceptions that could occur. We'll always want to close our connection to the database, so we will create a cursor (and do all the subsequent operations) inside a `try` block with `connection.close()` in a `finally` block (the `finally` block will get executed whether or not the `try` block succeeds).

The cursor is also a resource, so we'll grab one and use it in a `with:` block so that it'll automatically be closed when we're done with it. With the setup done, we can start executing the SQL code.

When we call the `cursor.execute()` function, the SQL code we will pass in will be run using the database engine, and the cursor will be populated with results if they are appropriate. We'll discuss later how we can read and write data using the cursor and the `execute()` function.

Creating the database

SQL reads similarly to English, so it's normally quite straightforward to work out what the existing SQL code does, even if it's a bit trickier to write new code. Our first SQL statement creates a `crimemap` database if it doesn't already exist (this means that if we come back to this script, we can leave this line in without deleting the entire database every time). We will create our first SQL statement as a string and use the `sql` variable to store it. Then, we will execute the statement using the cursor we created.

Looking at our table columns

Now that we know we have a database, we can create a table. The table will store the data for all the crimes that we record, with each crime in a row of the table. Therefore, we need several columns. Each column can be seen in our `create table` statement along with the type of data that will be stored in this column. To break these down, we have:

- **id**: This is a unique number that's automatically recorded for every crime we have. We don't need to worry too much about this field as MySQL will automatically insert it for us every time we add new crime data—starting at 1 and incrementing as required.

- **Latitude and longitude**: These fields will be used to store the location of each crime. We will specify `(10, 6)` after the floats which means that each float can be up to 10 digits and up to 6 digits can be after the decimal point.

- **Date**: This is the date and time of the crime.

- **Category**: We will define several categories to classify different types of crime. This will help in filtering the crimes later. VARCHAR(50) means that this will be data of variable length and up to 50 characters long.

- **Description**: This is similar to Category but with a maximum of 1000 characters.

- **Updated_at**: This is another field that we don't need to worry about. MySQL will set this to the current time when we insert the data or edit it. This could be useful if we want to, for example, remove a bunch of data that was inserted by mistake at a specific time.

Indexing and committing

The last line of our create table query specifies our id column as a *primary key*. This means that it'll be indexed (and therefore, we'll be able to find data very efficiently if we use it when we query our database), and will have various other useful properties, such as enforced existence and uniqueness.

Once we define this more complicated piece of SQL, we will execute it as well in the following line. Then, we will commit our changes to the database. Think of this as saving our changes; if we close the connection without the commit, our changes will be discarded.

SQL Commit:

> Forgetting to commit changes is a common error of SQL beginners. If you get to a point where your database doesn't behave as expected and you can't figure out why, check whether you forgot a commit somewhere in your code.

Using the database setup script

Save our script locally and push it to the repository. Refer to the following commands in this sequence:

```
git add db_setup.py
git commit -m "database setup script"
git push origin master
```

SSH to your VPS and clone the new repository to your /var/www directory using the following commands:

```
ssh user@123.456.789.123
cd /var/www
git clone <your-git-url>
cd crimemap
```

Adding credentials to our setup script

Now, we still don't have the credentials that our script relies on. We'll do two things before using our setup script:

- Create the dbconfig.py file with a database and password
- Add this file to .gitignore to prevent it from being added to our repository

Create and edit the dbconfig.py file directly on your VPS using nano, as follows:

```
nano dbconfig.py
```

Then, type the following using the password you chose when you installed MySQL:

```
db_user = "root"
db_password = "<your-mysql-password>"
```

Save it by hitting *Ctrl* + *X* and entering *Y* when prompted.

Now, use similar nano commands to create, edit, and save .gitignore, which should contain the following:

```
dbconfig.py
*.pyc
```

The first line prevents our dbconfig file from being added to our Git repository, which helps prevent an unauthorized use of our database password. The second line prevents compiled Python files from being added to the repository as these are simply runtime optimizations and are relevant to our project.

Running our database setup script

With this done, you can run:

```
python db_setup.py
```

Assuming everything goes smoothly, you should now have a database with a table to store crimes. Python will output any SQL errors, allowing you to debug if necessary. If you make changes to the script from the server, run the same git add, git commit, and git push commands that you did from your local machine.

git status:

 You can run `git status` from the terminal (make sure you are in your repository directory) to see a summary of the files that are committed. You could use this now (before `git push`) to make sure that you didn't commit the `dbconfig` file.

This concludes our preliminary database setup! Now, we can create a basic Flask project that uses our database.

Creating a basic database web application

We will start by building a skeleton of our Crime Map application. It'll be a basic Flask application with a single page that:

- Displays all the data in the `crimes` table of our database
- Allows users to input data and stores this data in the database
- Has a **Clear** button that deletes all the previously input data

Although what we will store and display can't really be described as *crime data* yet, we'll store it in the `crimes` table that we created earlier. We'll just use the `description` field for now, ignoring all the other ones.

The process of setting up the Flask application is very similar to what we did before. We will separate out the database logic into a separate file, leaving our main `crimemap.py` file for the Flask setup and routing.

Setting up our directory structure

On your local machine, change to the `crimemap` directory. If you created the database setup script on the server or made any changes to it there, make sure to sync the changes locally. Then, create the `templates` directory and touch the files we will use by running the following commands (or using the GUI file explorer if you prefer):

```
cd crimemap
git pull origin master
mkdir templates
touch templates/home.html
touch crimemap.py
touch dbhelper.py
```

Looking at our application code

Add the following code to the `crimemap.py` file. This contains nothing unexpected and should all be familiar from our Headlines project. The only thing to point out is the `DBHelper()` class, which we'll consider the code for next. We will simply create a global `DBHelper` instance right after initializing our application and then use it in the relevant methods to grab data from the database, insert data into the database, or delete all data from the database:

```python
from dbhelper import DBHelper
from flask import Flask
from flask import render_template
from flask import request


app = Flask(__name__)
DB = DBHelper()


@app.route("/")
def home():
    try:
        data = DB.get_all_inputs()
    except Exception as e:
        print e
        data = None
    return render_template("home.html", data=data)


@app.route("/add", methods=["POST"])
def add():
  try:
    data = request.form.get("userinput")
    DB.add_input(data)
  except Exception as e:
    print e
  return home()

@app.route("/clear")
def clear():
  try:
    DB.clear_all()
  except Exception as e:
    print e
  return home()

if __name__ == '__main__':
  app.run(port=5000, debug=True)
```

Looking at our SQL code

There's a little bit more SQL to learn from our database helper code. Add the following code to the dbhelper.py file:

```
import pymysql
import dbconfig


class DBHelper:

  def connect(self, database="crimemap"):
    return pymysql.connect(host='localhost',
              user=dbconfig.db_user,
              passwd=dbconfig.db_password,
              db=database)

  def get_all_inputs(self):
  connection = self.connect()
    try:
      query = "SELECT description FROM crimes;"
      with connection.cursor() as cursor:
        cursor.execute(query)
      return cursor.fetchall()
    finally:
      connection.close()

  def add_input(self, data):
    connection = self.connect()
    try:
      # The following introduces a deliberate security flaw.
      See section on SQL injection below
      query = "INSERT INTO crimes (description) VALUES
      ('{}');".format(data)
      with connection.cursor() as cursor:
        cursor.execute(query)
        connection.commit()
    finally:
      connection.close()


  def clear_all(self):
    connection = self.connect()
    try:
      query = "DELETE FROM crimes;"
      with connection.cursor() as cursor:
        cursor.execute(query)
        connection.commit()
    finally:
      connection.close()
```

As in our setup script, we need to make a connection with our database and then get a cursor from our connection in order to do anything meaningful. Again, we will do all our operations in `try: finally:` blocks in order to ensure that the connection is closed.

In our helper, we will consider three of the four main database operations. **CRUD** (**Create, Read, Update,** and **Delete**) describes the basic database operations. We will either create and insert new data, read the existing data, modify the existing data, or delete the existing data. We have no need to update data in our basic app, but creating, reading, and deleting are certainly useful.

Reading data

Let's start with reading, assuming that there is some data already in our database. In SQL, this is done using the `SELECT` statement; we will choose which data we want to retrieve based on a set of conditions. In our case, the query in the `get_all_inputs` function is `SELECT description FROM crimes;`. We'll take a look a bit later at how to refine a `SELECT` query, but this one just grabs the `description` field for every row in our `crimes` table. This is similar to the example we talked about at the beginning of this chapter, in which we wanted to send out a newsletter and needed the e-mail address of each of our customers. Here, we want the description of each of our crimes.

Once the cursor executes the query, it will point to the beginning of a data structure containing the results. We will perform `fetchall()` on our cursor, which transforms our results set to a list so that we can pass them back to our application code. (If you've used generators in Python, it may help to think of a database cursor as a generator. It knows how to iterate over the data but doesn't itself contain all the data).

Inserting data

Next up is our `add_input()` function. This takes the data input by the user and *inserts* it into the database. Creating data in SQL is done using the `INSERT` keyword. Our query (assuming `foobar` is our passed in data) is `INSERT into crimes (description) VALUES ('foobar')`.

This may look overcomplicated for what it actually does, but remember that we're still dealing with a single field (description). We'll discuss later how `INSERT` is designed to accept multiple but arbitrary columns, which can all be named in the first set of brackets, and then matching values for each of these, which are given in the second set of brackets, after `VALUES`.

As we made changes to the database, we will need to *commit* our connection to make these permanent.

Deleting data

Finally, we will take a look at how concise a `DELETE` statement in SQL can be. `DELETE FROM crimes` wipes all the data from our `crimes` database. We'll consider later how to make this keyword behave less like a nuke by specifying conditions to delete only some data.

Again, this makes changes to our database, so we need to commit these.

If all the new SQL commands seem to be a lot to take in, go play around with them for a bit in an online sandbox or even in our own live SQL shell that we discussed how to access earlier. You'll find that SQL comes quite naturally after a while as most of its keywords are taken from a natural language, and it uses very few symbols.

Finally, let's take a look at our HTML template.

Creating our view code

Python and SQL are fun to write, and they are indeed the main part of our application. However, at the moment, we have a house without doors or windows; the difficult and impressive bit is done, but it's unusable. Let's add a few lines of HTML to allow the world to interact without the code we wrote.

In `templates/home.html`, add the following:

```html
<html>
<body>
  <head>
    <title>Crime Map</title>
  </head>

  <h1>Crime Map</h1>
  <form action="/add" method="POST">
    <input type="text" name="userinput">
    <input type="submit" value="Submit">
    </form>
  <a href="/clear">clear</a>
  {% for userinput in data %}
    <p>{{userinput}}</p>
    {% endfor %}
</body>
</html>
```

There's nothing we haven't seen before. Here, we had a form with a single text input to add data to our database by calling the /add function of our app, and directly below it, we looped through all the existing data and displayed each piece within <p> tags.

Running the code on our VPS

Finally, we need to make our code accessible to the world. This means pushing it to our git repo, pulling it onto the VPS, and configuring Apache to serve it. Run the following commands locally:

```
git add .
git commit -m "Skeleton CrimeMap"
git push origin master
ssh <username>@<vps-ip-address>
```

Now, on your VPS, run the following:

```
cd /var/www/crimemap
git pull origin master
```

Now, we need a .wsgi file to link Python to Apache, which can be created by running the following command:

```
nano crimemap.wsgi
```

The .wsgi file should contain the following:

```
import sys
sys.path.insert(0, "/var/www/crimemap")
from crimemap import app as application
```

Now, hit *Ctrl* + *X* and then enter *Y* when prompted to save.

We also need to create a new Apache .conf file, and to set this as the default (instead of headlines, the .conf file that is our current default). Run the following commands to create the file:

```
cd /etc/apache2/sites-available
nano crimemap.conf
```

Next, add the following code:

```
<VirtualHost *>
    ServerName example.com

    WSGIScriptAlias / /var/www/crimemap/crimemap.wsgi
```

```
    WSGIDaemonProcess crimemap
    <Directory /var/www/crimemap>
       WSGIProcessGroup crimemap
       WSGIApplicationGroup %{GLOBAL}
        Order deny,allow
        Allow from all
    </Directory>
  </VirtualHost>
```

This is so similar to the `headlines.conf` file we created for our previous project that you might find it easier to just copy the previous one and substitute as necessary.

Finally, we need to deactivate the old site and activate the new one, as follows:

```
sudo a2dissite headlines.conf
sudo a2ensite crimemap.conf
sudo service apache2 reload
```

Now, everything should be working. If you copied the code out manually, it's almost certain that there's a bug or two to deal with. Don't be discouraged by this; remember that debugging is expected to be a large part of development! If necessary, run `tail -f /var/log/apache2/error.log` while you load the site to note any errors. If this fails, add some print statements to `crimemap.py` and `dbhelper.py` to narrow down where things are breaking.

Once everything works, you should be able to see a web page with a single text input. When you submit text through the input, you should see the text displayed on the page, as in the example that follows:

Note how the data we get from the database is a tuple, so it is surrounded by brackets and has a trailing comma. This is because we selected only a single field, `'description'`, from our `crimes` table, while we could, in theory, be dealing with many columns for each crime (and soon we will do so).

Mitigating against SQL injection

Our application contains a fatal flaw. We take input from our users and insert it into our SQL statements using Python string formatting. This works well when the user enters a normal alphanumeric string as expected, but if the user is malicious, they can actually inject their own SQL code and take control of our database. Although SQL injection is an old attack and most modern technology automatically mitigates against it, there are still dozens of attacks against major corporations every year in which passwords or financial data are leaked due to a SQL injection vulnerability. We'll take a moment to discuss what an SQL injection is and how to prevent it.

Injecting SQL into our database application

Navigate to our web application and hit the **clear** link to remove any saved inputs. Now, in the input, type `Bobby` and click on the **Submit** button. The page should now look similar to the following image:

In this input, now type:

```
'); DELETE FROM crimes; --
```

All characters are important here.

The input needs to start with a single quote followed by a close bracket, followed by a semicolon, and then followed by the delete statement, another semicolon, a space, and finally two hyphens. You might expect to see a second line when the page refreshes, listing this strange-looking string beneath the **Bobby** output, but instead, you'll see a blank page that looks similar to the screenshot that follows:

This is weird, right? Let's take a look at what happened. In our DBHelper class, our insert statements have the following line:

```
query = "INSERT INTO crimes (description) VALUES
('{}');".format(data)
```

This means that the user's input gets added into the SQL code just before we run the code on the database. When we put the strange-looking input that we used previously into the placeholder of the SQL statement, we will get the following string:

```
"INSERT INTO crimes (description) VALUES (''); DELETE FROM crimes; --
');"
```

These are two SQL statements instead of one. We closed off the INSERT statement with an empty value and then deleted everything in the crimes table with the DELETE statement. The two hyphens at the end form an SQL comment so that the extra close quotation mark and bracket don't cause any syntax errors. When we input our data, we inserted a blank row into our database and then deleted all the data from the crimes table!

Of course, a creative attacker could run any SQL statement in place of the DELETE statement that we chose. They could drop an entire table (refer to https://xkcd.com/327/ for a humorous example), or they could run a select statement to bypass a database login function. Alternatively, if you store credit card information, a similar attack could be used to fetch the data and display it to the attacker. In general, we don't want the users of our web application to be able to run arbitrary code on our database!

Mitigating against SQL injection

Mitigating against SQL injection involves sanitizing user inputs and making sure that if the user inputs special characters that might be interpreted as SQL syntax, these characters are ignored. There are different ways to do this, and we'll use a simple one provided automatically by our Python SQL library. For more comprehensive information on this topic, take a look at https://www.owasp.org/index.php/SQL_Injection_Prevention_Cheat_Sheet.

In the dbhelper.py file, change the add_input() method to read as follows:

```
def add_input(self, data):
    connection = self.connect()
  try:
      query = "INSERT INTO crimes (description) VALUES (%s);"
      with connection.cursor() as cursor:
          cursor.execute(query, data)
          connection.commit()
      finally:
          connection.close()
```

The %s token that we used here is a string placeholder similar to %d, which is used in normal Python strings as a placeholder and an older alternative to braces. However, instead of using Python's str.format() function, we will pass the string and values that we want to insert into the placeholders to the PyMySQL cursor.execute() function. This will now automatically escape all characters that are meaningful to SQL so that we don't have to worry about them being executed.

Now, if you try the inputs again, you'll see them displayed as expected-special characters and all-as in the screenshot that follows:

In the final chapter of this book, we'll briefly talk about ORM techniques that can provide even stronger mitigation against SQL injection attacks. While it might seem to be a simple problem that we've solved by escaping some special characters, it can actually become quite subtle. Tools such as **sqlmap** (`http://sqlmap.org/`) can try hundreds of different variants on the same idea (that is, the idea of inputting special characters against a database) until one gets unexpected results and a vulnerability is found. Remember that for your application to be secure, it has to be protected against every possible vulnerability; for it to be insecure, it only has to be vulnerable to one.

Summary

That's it for the introduction to our Crime Map project. We discussed how to install a MySQL database on our VPS and how to hook it up to Flask. We looked at creating, reading, updating, and deleting data, and we created a basic database web application that can accept user input and display it back again. We finished off by looking at the SQL injection vulnerability and how to protect ourselves against it.

Next up, we'll add a Google Maps widget and some better aesthetics.

7
Adding Google Maps to Our Crime Map Project

In the previous chapter, we set up a database and discussed how to add and remove data from it through Flask. With a web application that can do input and output with long-term storage, we now have the building blocks needed for nearly all web applications and are limited only by the power of our imagination.

In this chapter, we will add more features than the text-only interface from the previous chapter; we'll add embedded Google Maps that will allow a user to view and select geographic coordinates in an intuitive way.

Google Maps is written in JavaScript, and we'll need to write some JavaScript code to adapt Google Maps to our needs. As always, we'll do a whirlwind tutorial for readers who haven't ever used JavaScript before, but if you're interested in solidifying your all-inclusive web application knowledge, now is a good time to quickly go through a couple of JavaScript-specific tutorials. If you've never seen any JavaScript code before, an easy introduction that is similar to the HTML and CSS tutorials we provided links to before can be found at `http://www.w3schools.com/js/default.asp`.

Arguably, the most important part of a crime map is the map itself. We'll use the Google Maps API, which is simple and powerful for developers and intuitive for users. As a first step, we'll just add a basic map that loads to an area and zoom level that we choose. Once we've seen to this, we'll add functionality to allow for markers. Markers will serve two purposes for our map: first, we'll display a marker on the map in the location of every crime we have saved in our database; second, when the user clicks on the map, it'll add a new marker and allow the user to submit a new crime report (eventually by adding a description and date in form fields).

However, first we need to be able to run our application locally again for development and debugging. Having linked it to the database, this is a bit tricky; so, we'll look at how to solve this common problem.

In this chapter, we'll cover the following topics:

- Running a database application locally
- Adding an embedded Google Map widget to our application
- Adding an input form for new crimes
- Displaying existing crimes on our map

Running a database application locally

In order to develop and debug locally, we need to be able to run the application. However, at the moment, this is not possible as MySQL is only installed on our VPS. There are three main options to develop our database application locally:

- Connecting to the database on our VPS even when running Flask on our local machine
- Installing MySQL on our local machine
- Creating a "mock" of our database in memory using Python

While any could work, we'll go with the third option. Connecting to our production database would cause us to be affected by latency if we develop in a location far from our VPS, and this would also mean that we'd run test code against our production database, which is never a good idea. The second option would limit the portability of our development environment, increase setup time if we switch to a new development environment, and in the worst case scenario, use up a significant amount of local resources.

Creating a mock of our database

If you try to run the `crimemap.py` file locally, the first error you will see is `ImportError` because of the `dbconfig.py` file that we don't have. In the previous chapter, we created this file directly on our VPS and didn't check it into git as it contained sensitive database credentials. We'll create a local copy of `dbconfig.py`, which indicates that our application should use a mock database. We'll update the `dbconfig.py` file on our VPS to indicate that the real database should be used when the app is run from there. We'll do this with a simple Boolean flag.

Adding a test flag

In your local `crimemap` directory, create a new `dbconfig.py` file and add a single line of code:

```
test = True
```

Now, SSH into your VPS and add the flag to the production configuration as well; although, here, the value should be set to `False`, as follows:

ssh user@123.456.789.123

cd /var/www/crimemap

nano dbconfig.py

Add the following to the top of the file:

```
test = False
```

Then, type *Ctrl + X* followed by *Y* to save and quit the file

Now, exit the SSH session. This will solve `ImportError` (the `dbconfig.py` file now exists on our VPS and locally), and our application is now aware of whether it is running in test or production.

Writing the mock code

Our flag doesn't actually do anything yet though, and we don't want to trigger all the exceptions when we test our app. Instead, we'll write a "mock" of our database code (the code in the `dbhelper.py` file) that'll return basic static data or `None`. When our application runs, it will be able to call database functions normally, but there will be no actual database. Instead, we'll have a few lines of Python to emulate a very basic database. Create the `mockdbhelper.py` file in your `crimemap` directory and add the following code:

```python
class MockDBHelper:

    def connect(self, database="crimemap"):
        pass

    def get_all_inputs(self):
        return []

    def add_input(self, data):
        pass

    def clear_all(self):
        pass
```

As you can note, the methods we used for our basic database application all exist but don't do anything. The get_all_inputs() method returns an empty list, which we can still pass to our template. Now, we just need to tell our app to use this instead of the real DBHelper class if we are in a testing environment. Add the following code to the end of the imports section in crimemap.py, making sure to remove the existing import for DBHelper:

```
import dbconfig
if dbconfig.test:
    from mockdbhelper import MockDBHelper as DBHelper
else:
    from dbhelper import DBHelper
```

We use our test flag in dbconfig to specify whether or not to import the real DBHelper (which relies on having a connection to MySQL) or to import the mock DBHelper (which does not need database connection). If we import the mock helper, we can change the name so that the rest of the code can continue to run without conditional checks for the test flag.

Validating our expectations

Now, you should be able to run the code locally, just as before we added a database dependency. In your terminal, run:

python crimemap.py

Then, visit localhost:5000 in your browser to take a look at your app loading. Check the output of the terminal to make sure that no exceptions are triggered (as would be the case if you attempted to run the real DBHelper code instead of the mock ones we just made). Although our application no longer "works", we can at least run it to test our code that doesn't involve the database. Then, when we deploy to production, everything should work exactly as in our tests, but with a real database plugged in.

Adding an embedded Google Maps widget to our application

Now, we want to add a map view to our app instead of the basic input box. Google Maps allows you to create a map without registration, but you will only be able to make a limited number of API calls. If you create this project, publish a link on the Web, and it goes viral, you stand a chance of hitting the limit (which is currently 2,500 map loads per day). If you think this will be a limiting factor, you can register for the maps API and have the option of paying Google for more capacity. However, the free version will be more than adequate for development and even production if your app isn't too popular.

Adding the map to our template

We want to display a map on the main page of our app, so this means editing the code in the `home.html` file in our `templates` directory. Remove all the existing code and replace it with the following:

```
<!DOCTYPE html>
<html lang="en">
  <head>
    <script type="text/javascript"
      src="https://maps.googleapis.com/maps/api/js">
    </script>

    <script type="text/javascript">
      function initialize() {
        var mapOptions = {
          center: new google.maps.LatLng(-
          33.30578381949298, 26.523442268371582),
          zoom: 15
        };
        var map = new
        google.maps.Map(document.getElementById("map-
          canvas"),mapOptions);
      }
    </script>

  </head>
    <body onload="initialize()">
    <div id="map-canvas" style="width:80%;
      height:500px;"></div>
    </body>
</html>
```

Introducing JavaScript

Let's take a look at what happened here. The first line told our user's browser that we're using HTML5. Lines 4 to 6 include the map resources we need in our page. Note that this is between `<script>` tags, indicating that it's JavaScript. In this particular case, we did not actually write the JavaScript code – we simply linked to where it's hosted on Google's servers. Think of this a bit as a Python `import` statement, except we don't even have to install the package locally; it's simply "imported" at runtime by your user's browser.

Directly following this is our setup script to display a basic map. Again, this is between `<script>` tags to indicate that it's JavaScript instead of HTML. This time, we actually wrote the JavaScript code ourselves though. The syntax is similar to Java in terms of brackets, braces, and `for` loops. Apart from this and its name, there is little relation between it and Java.

The first line of our JavaScript code is a function definition; similar to Python's "`def`" we use the `function` keyword to define a new function named `initialise()`. We declared a variable with `var mapOptions =` and assigned a new JavaScript object to this variable that looks similar to a Python dictionary. We define a location with a latitude-longitude tuple-like object, which we have access to because of Lines 4 to 6, and the object also contains a "`zoom`" level. These options describe our initial map: which area should be displayed and at what zoom level.

Finally, we created a new variable, `map`, and initialized a Google map object, passing in the ID of an HTML element (which we'll explain in more detail in the following section) and the map options we just defined. We then reached the end of our JavaScript code, so we closed the `<script>` tag.

The body of our HTML code

Although our `<body>` section is only a couple of lines, it has some subtleties. The first line opens the `<body>` tag and also defines the `onload` parameter. This parameter takes the name of a JavaScript function that will be called automatically when the page is loaded. Note that the function name ("`initialize`", in our case, as this is the function we just wrote and want to be run automatically in order to create our map) is enclosed in inverted commas. This might be counterintuitive if you think of Python, in which inverted commas are used mainly for string literals. Think of it as passing the function *name* to the body block but note the fact that we still use the open-close brackets as part of the name.

The next line creates a `<div>` element. Normally, `<div>` does nothing except enclose more HTML, but this doesn't mean that an empty `<div>` block, as we have here, is pointless. Note the ID, `map-canvas`, that we give our `<div>`. This matches the name in our JavaScript code; that is, the JavaScript function will look for an HTML element called `map-canvas` (using `document.getElementById()`) and transform this into Google Maps widget. Therefore, it makes sense to use a `<div>` element as we want an empty element for our JavaScript code to use.

Finally, our `<div>` element also includes some inline CSS. We can define the width and height of our map (which is a requirement of the Google Maps API) using CSS's `height` and `width` attributes. In this case, we defined the map to a constant `height` value of `500` pixels and a `width` value of `80%` of the page. The percentage for the width is useful as the scrolling functionality is often overloaded with the zoom functionality. That is, if the user wants to scroll down on our page using a touchpad or mouse wheel and his or her cursor is over the map, the map will zoom in instead of the page scrolling down. The 20 percent "blank" space on the right-hand side, therefore, provides the user with somewhere to move the mouse to while scrolling. Similarly, for touchscreens, the user would "*pan*" around the map while trying to scroll, but can use this space to put his or her finger while scrolling.

Testing and debugging

We should now be able to run our web app locally and see the embedded Google Map. If your app is not already running, use your terminal to start it up again and navigate to `localhost:5000` in your browser. As we don't store the code for Google Maps locally, this needs to be fetched from Google's servers, so we need our local machine to be online for this to work (similar to fetching the data we needed for our Headlines application).

Debugging JavaScript code is a bit tricky as any errors won't be registered by Flask and will therefore not be seen in your app output. If your web page is blank or does anything unexpected, the first place to look is your browser's developer console. This is a developer's tool that can be found in all the major browsers, normally by pressing *Ctrl + Shift + C* and navigating to the "**Console**" tab in the window or sidebar that appears. Here, you'll note any JavaScript errors or warnings that your code has triggered, so this tool is invaluable in debugging a web application.

Although the console should report line numbers along with errors, it can sometimes be difficult to track down exactly what is going wrong. JavaScript is a dynamically typed language and is infamous for having some pretty quirky and counterintuitive behavior. If necessary, you can also add JavaScript lines between the `<script>` tags in your HTML that do nothing but log in to the developer tools console. To do this, use the following:

```
console.log("A message");
```

This is similar to a Python `print` statement, and you can pass variables and most objects to see a string representation of them logged to the output. Use the + symbol to concatenate. For example, if you have a variable named "a" and you want to see its value at a specific point in code, you could add the following line:

```
console.log("The value of a is: " + a);
```

For a more sophisticated approach to debugging, take a look at the **Debugger** tab of the developer tools window (or its equivalent in your browser) and play around with setting breakpoints in JavaScript. The developer tools are generally a powerful suite of tools and their full functionality is unfortunately beyond the scope of this book. The following screenshot shows the Mozilla Firefox developer console with a breakpoint set just before the map loads:

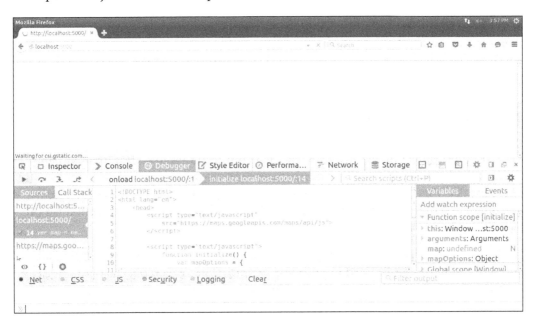

Once all the bugs are squashed (or straight-away if you are meticulous and lucky), you should see a page in your browser containing an embedded Google Map centered on **Grahamstown**, South Africa. Play around with the zoom level and coordinates set by the mapOptions variable in your JavaScript code to get the initial map of your choice. Clicking and holding on the map will allow "panning" or moving around the world. Zooming is done by scrolling with your middle mouse wheel, using your touchpad, or "pinch zooming" on touchscreen. The result should look similar to the following screenshot:

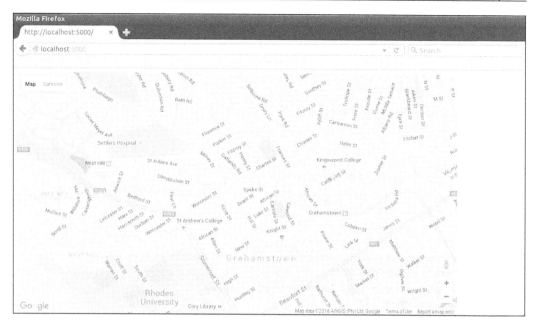

Let's now move on to making our map more interactive and useful.

Making our map interactive

The first functionality we'll add to our app will allow the user to place a marker on the map. This will eventually allow the user to add a crime report by indicating where the crime took place, thus adding to our crowd-sourced database of crimes. We'll implement the marker functionality in JavaScript, as well, using a "listener".

Adding markers

JavaScript is *event-driven*. Actions such as a mouse move or mouse click are events, and we can react to these events by setting up an event listener. The listener simply runs in the background, waiting for a specific event, and then triggers a specified action if it detects the event. We'll set up a listener for a mouse click, and if detected, we'll place a map marker at the location of the mouse when clicked.

Using the Google Map API, this can be achieved in a few lines of code. First, we'll make our `map` variable global. Then, we'll create a `placeMarker()` function that will reference our `map` variable and place a marker on it when called. In our existing `initalise()` function, we'll add a click listener that will call the `placeMarker()` function when triggered.

The full JavaScript code can be seen here with the modified lines highlighted:

```html
<script type="text/javascript"
  src="https://maps.googleapis.com/maps/api/js">
</script>

<script type="text/javascript">

  var map;
  function initialize() {
  var mapOptions = {
    center: new google.maps.LatLng(-33.30578381949298,
      26.523442268371582),
    zoom: 15
  };
  map = new google.maps.Map(document.getElementById("map-
    canvas"), mapOptions);
  google.maps.event.addListener(map, 'click',
    function(event){
    placeMarker(event.latLng);
    });
  }

  function placeMarker(location) {
  var marker = new google.maps.Marker({
    position: location,
    map: map
  });
  }
</script>
```

Note specifically the change from `var map = new google.maps.Map` to `map = new google.maps.Map`. We removed the `var` declaration, which means that we assigned our new map to our global `map` variable instead of creating a new local variable.

The next line makes a call to `addListener()`, which might look a little odd. The `addListener()` function takes a `map`, `event`, and `function` to be called when the listener is triggered. As in Python, JavaScript has first-class functions, which means that we can pass functions as arguments to other functions. Unlike Python, we don't need to use the `lambda` keyword to create an anonymous function; we can simply declare the function we want to pass in place of the argument. In this case, we created an anonymous function that takes an `event` argument and in turn calls our `placeMarker()` function, passing it the `latLng` property of `event`. In our case, `event` is the mouse click that is picked up by the listener, and the `latLng` property is the location of the mouse click.

In our `placeMarker()` function, we accepted a location and created a new `Marker` object, placing it at the passed-in location on our map (this is why we made the map global; now we can refer to it in this new function).

In summary, when the page loads, we will add a listener that hangs around in the background, waiting for a click. When a click is detected, the listener makes a call to `placeMarker()`, passing in the coordinates of the click it detected. The `placeMarker()` function then adds a marker at the specified coordinates, meaning that the user sees a marker appear on the map as he or she clicks on the map. Give it a try, using the console and debugger in your browser, as we did before, if things don't go as expected. You should see a new marker placed on the map for every click and be able to generate maps that look similar to the following screenshot:

Using a single marker

Creating a new marker for every click is not ideal. We actually want the user to be able to move the marker with each click instead of creating a new one. Adding more than one crime at a time would be overcomplicated and not overly useful.

To achieve this, create another global `marker` variable under the existing global `map` variable. Then, add a simple condition to the `placeMarker()` function that creates a new marker only if there isn't one already and moves the location of the existing one otherwise.

The full code, again with the modified lines highlighted, is shown as follows. Again, note that we removed `var` from the line where we created a new `marker` variable, thus using the global variable instead of creating a local one. With these changes, each click on the map should move the marker instead of creating a new one. Try it out:

```
<script type="text/javascript"
  src="https://maps.googleapis.com/maps/api/js">
</script>

<script type="text/javascript">

  var map;
  var marker;
  function initialize() {
    var mapOptions = {
    center: new google.maps.LatLng(-33.30578381949298,
      26.523442268371582),
    zoom: 15
    };
    map = new google.maps.Map(document.getElementById("map-
      canvas"), mapOptions);
    google.maps.event.addListener(map, 'click',
     function(event){
       placeMarker(event.latLng);
     });
  }

  function placeMarker(location) {
    if (marker) {
      marker.setPosition(location);
    } else {
     marker = new google.maps.Marker({
       position: location,
       map: map
     });
    }
  }
</script>
```

Adding an input form for new crimes

We want the user to be able to specify more information than simply a location. The next step is to create a form that the user can use to add date, category, and description data to a crime submission. Each of these pieces of information will be stored in the database columns we created in the previous chapter. Creating web forms is a common enough task that there are many frameworks and plugins to help automate as much of the process as possible, as most forms need a pretty frontend, which includes error messages if the user puts in unexpected input, as well as backend logic to process the data and do a more thorough validation to prevent malformed or incorrect data from polluting the database

However, in the spirit of learning, we'll now create the backend and frontend of a web form from scratch. In our next project, we'll take a look at how to do something similar using various tools to make the process less laborious.

Our goal is to have a number of input fields to the right of our map, which allows the user to specify details about a witnessed or experienced crime and submit it to be included with our existing data. The form should have the following inputs:

- **Category**: A drop-down menu that allows the user to select which category the crime falls into
- **Date**: A calendar that allows the user to easily enter the date and time of the crime
- **Description**: A larger text box that allows the user to describe the crime in free-form text
- **Latitude and Longitude**: Text boxes that are automatically populated based on the location selected using the marker

After filling the preceding fields, the user should be able to click on a **Submit** button and view the crime he or she just submitted appear on the map.

The HTML code for the form

The HTML code needed for our form is very similar to the forms created in our earlier project, but it has some new elements as well, namely `<textarea>` and `<label>` and an input with `type= "date"`. The `<textarea>` element is very similar to the standard text fields we noted before but appears as a larger square to encourage the user to enter more text. Label elements can define a `for` attribute to specify what we are labeling. The text between the opening and closing `label` tags is then shown close to the element to be labeled.

This is useful for our form as we can prompt the user about what data to enter in each field. The date field will provide a nice calendar drop-down menu to select a date. Unfortunately, it's a fairly recent addition to HTML and is not supported in all browsers. In unsupported browsers (including Firefox), this will be identical to a text input, so we'll look at how to handle dates input by the user at the end of this chapter.

Also, note that we put the form inside a `<div>` element to make it easier to style and position on the page (we'll also do this later). The full `<body>` element of our HTML page now looks as follows (note that we added a heading and paragraph above the map, while the form is added below the map). Take a look at the following code:

```
<body onload="initialize()">
  <h1>CrimeMap</h1>
  <p>A map of recent criminal activity in the
   Grahamstown area.</p>
  <div id="map-canvas" style="width:70%;
   height:500px"></div>

  <div id="newcrimeform">
   <h2>Submit new crime</h2>
   <form action="/submitcrime" method="POST">
    <label for="category">Category</label>
    <select name="category" id="category">
     <option value="mugging">Mugging</option>
     <option value="breakin">Break-in</option>
    </select>
    <label for="date">Date</label>
    <input name="date" id="date" type="date">
    <label for="latitude">Latitude</label>
    <input name="latitude" id="latitude"
     type="text">
    <label for="longitude">Longitude</label>
    <input name="longitude" id="longitude"
     type="text">
    <label for="description">Description</label>
    <textarea name="description" id="description"
       placeholder="A brief but detailed
     description of the crime"></textarea>
    <input type="submit" value="Submit">
   </form>
  </div>
</body>
```

Refresh your page to see the form below the map. You'll notice that it looks pretty terrible with different-sized fields and a horizontal layout, as in the following screenshot:

Let's add some CSS to fix this.

Adding external CSS to our web application

To make the form appear to the right of our map, we'll use CSS. We already have some CSS for our map, and we could add more CSS in a similar way. However, refer to our discussion of inline, internal, and external CSS from *Chapter 5, Improving the User Experience of Our Headlines Project*, in the *Adding CSS to our Headlines application* section, and remember that having all CSS in a separate file is best practice. Therefore, we'll create a `style.css` file and consider how to link it to our Flask app.

Creating the CSS file in our directory structure

By default in Flask, our static files should be kept in a directory called `static`. We'll want to keep various kinds of files in here eventually, such as images, JavaScript, and CSS, so we'll create a subdirectory called `css` and create our `style.css` file inside this. Navigate to your project directory in your terminal and run the following to add this directory structure and file to our project:

```
mkdir -p static/css
touch static/css/style.css
```

Adding CSS code

Insert the following CSS code into this new file:

```css
body {
  font-family: sans-serif;
  background: #eee;
}

input, select, textarea {
  display: block;
  color: grey;
  border: 1px solid lightsteelblue;
  line-height: 15px;
  margin: 2px 6px 16px 0px;
  width: 100%;
}

input[type="submit"] {
  padding: 5px 10px 5px 10px;
  color: black;
  background: lightsteelblue;
  border: none;
  box-shadow: 1px 1px 1px #4C6E91;
}

input[type="submit"]:hover {
  background: steelblue;
}

#map-canvas {
  width: 70%;
  height: 500px;
  float: left;
```

```
}

#newcrimeform {
 float: right;
 width: 25%;
}
```

You'll probably notice the similarities with the CSS code that we used for our Headlines project. However, there are still some important points to note:

- We defined the `width` and `height` of any element with the ID of `map-canvas` here (in the second-last block), so we can remove the inline style from our `body.html` file.

- We used CSS's float functionality to display our form to the right of our map instead of below it. The map takes up `70%` of the `width` of the page, and the form takes up `25%` (with the last 5% left so that the map and form have some space between them. Our map floats to the left of the page, while the form floats to the right. Because they take up less than 100% of the width combined, they'll be displayed side by side in the browser.)

Configuring Flask to use CSS

Normally in HTML pages, we can link to external CSS files simply by giving a relative path to the stylesheet. As we're using Flask, we need to configure our application to return the CSS file as a static one. By default, Flask serves files from a directory named `static` in the route of the project, which is why it's important to place the CSS file here, as described earlier. Flask can generate a URL for the CSS file we need to link to using the `url_for` function. In the `home.html` template, add the following line to the top of the `<head>` section:

```
<link type="text/css" rel="stylesheet" href="{{url_for('static',
 filename='css/style.css') }}" />
```

This creates a link between our HTML and CSS. We used attributes to describe the link as being to a `text/css` file and that it is a stylesheet. We then gave its location with `href` using the `url_for()` function.

We also need to add a line of JavaScript code to populate the location input automatically whenever the marker on the map is created or moved. This is achieved by adding the lines highlighted in the following to the `placeMarker()` function:

```
function placeMarker(location) {
 if (marker) {
  marker.setPosition(location);
 } else {
```

```
    marker = new google.maps.Marker({
     position: location,
     map: map
    });
   }
   document.getElementById('latitude').value = location.lat();
   document.getElementById('longitude').value = location.lng();
   }
```

These lines simply find the latitude and longitude boxes (identified by their id attribute) and insert the location used to place the marker. When we POST the form to the server, we'll be able to read these values on the backend.

Finally, remove the inline CSS that we added earlier as this functionality is now the responsibility of our external stylesheet. Take a look at the following line in the home.html file:

```
<div id="map-canvas" style="width:70%; height:500px"></div>
```

The preceding line can be modified to instead be as follows:

```
<div id="map-canvas"></div>
```

Viewing the result

Reload the page in your browser to view the result. Remember that CSS and JavaScript are often cached by your browser, so hit *Ctrl + R* for a hard refresh if you see unexpected behavior. If *Ctrl + R* does not work, try hitting *Ctrl + Shift + Delete* and select the **cache** option in the browser's menu and clear the browsing data before refreshing again.

The styled map with the form should look similar to the following screenshot:

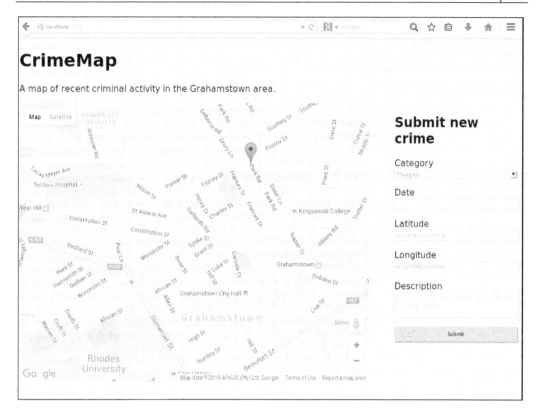

Note that clicking on the map now populates the latitude and longitude boxes with the coordinates of the marker.

Publishing the result

We have the form, the map, and some CSS, so now is a good time to push the result to our VPS so that we can see what it looks like on different devices or ask people for feedback.

To push our changes, fire up a terminal, change the directory to the root folder, and run the following:

```
git add crimemap.py
git add templates/home.html
git add static
git commit -m "Map with form and CSS"
git push origin master
```

Then, SSH into your VPS and pull the new code by running the following:

```
cd /var/www/crimemap
git pull origin master
sudo service apache2 reload
```

Visit the IP of your VPS to check whether the page worked and looks right. As usual, look at /var/log/apache2/error.log if anything unexpected happens.

Linking the form to the backend

It's all very well to have a pretty form to accept user input, but at the moment, we're just throwing away any submitted data. Instead of processing input in real time, as we did in our headlines application, we want to capture the input and store it in our database. Let's take a look at how to achieve this.

Setting up the URL to collect POST data

As in our Headlines project, the first step is to set up a URL on our server to which the data can be posted. In the HTML form we created, we set this URL to be /submitcrime, so let's create this as a route in our Flask app. In crimemap.py, add the following function:

```python
@app.route("/submitcrime", methods=['POST'])
def submitcrime():
 category = request.form.get("category")
 date = request.form.get("date")
 latitude = float(request.form.get("latitude"))
 longitude = float(request.form.get("longitude"))
 description = request.form.get("description")
 DB.add_crime(category, date, latitude, longitude, description)
 return home()
```

Here, we simply grabbed all the data the user entered and passed it to our database helper. We used the DB.add_crime() function in the preceding code, but this does not yet exist. We need it to really add the new data to our database for our real DBHelper, and we also need a stub of this function for MockDBHelper. Let's take a look at how to add these.

Adding the database methods

In `MockDBHelper.py`, the function is simple. It needs to take the same arguments and then not do anything. Add the following to `mockdbhelper.py`:

```
def add_crime(self, category, date, latitude, longitude,
    description):
  pass
```

The real function needs to be added to `dbhelper.py` and is a bit more involved. It looks:

```
def add_crime(self, category, date, latitude, longitude,
    description):
  connection = self.connect()
  try:
    query = "INSERT INTO crimes (category, date, latitude,
      longitude, description) \
      VALUES (%s, %s, %s, %s, %s)"
    with connection.cursor() as cursor:
      cursor.execute(query, (category, date, latitude, longitude,
description))
      connection.commit()
  except Exception as e:
    print(e)
  finally:
    connection.close()
```

There is nothing we haven't seen before here. We used placeholder values and only populated them within the `cursor.execute()` statement to avoid SQL injection, and we closed our connection in a `finally` block to make sure it always happens.

Testing the code on the server

Here is another good point to commit all the changes to the repository and do a quick check for bugs. Once the new code runs on your VPS, try adding a crime to the database by visiting your IP address and filling in the form we made. On your VPS, you can check to make sure the data was successfully added by running the following commands. Note that this fires up a live SQL shell—a direct connection to your database that should be used with care. A mistyped command can result in data being irretrievably lost or corrupted. Run the following:

```
mysql -p
<your database password>
use database crimemap
select * from crimes;
```

You'll see that MySQL prints a nice ASCII table that shows a summary of the data in your database, as in the following screenshot (in this case, all the records and columns from the `crimes` table of the `crimemap` database are shown):

```
mysql> select * from crimes;
+----+-----------+-----------+---------------------+----------+---------------+---------------------+
| id | latitude  | longitude | date                | category | description   | updated_at          |
+----+-----------+-----------+---------------------+----------+---------------+---------------------+
| 19 | -33.307438| 26.522497 | 2016-03-03 00:00:00 | mugging  | test 1        | 2016-02-27 04:58:30 |
| 20 | -33.308372| 26.523701 | 2100-01-01 00:00:00 | mugging  | Thought Crime | 2016-02-27 04:58:54 |
+----+-----------+-----------+---------------------+----------+---------------+---------------------+
2 rows in set (0.00 sec)
```

Displaying existing crimes on our map

Now, the user can add new crimes to our crime database, but we want the map to display crimes that are already added as well. To achieve this, whenever the page is loaded, our app needs to make a call to the database to get the latest crime data. We then need to pass this data to our template file, loop through each crime, and place a marker in the correct place on the map.

Now, our data is stored in a MySQL database. We will access it using Python on the server side, and we want to display it using JavaScript on the client side; so, we'll need to spend a bit of time on converting our data to the appropriate format. When we access the data through our Python `pymysql` driver, we will receive it as a tuple. To display the data using JavaScript, we want it in JSON. JSON, you might remember from our Headlines project, is JavaScript Object Notation, a structured data format that JavaScript can easily read and manipulate. As with our previous project, we'll take advantage of the fact that Python dictionaries are very similar to JSON. We'll create a Python dictionary from the tuple we get out of our database, convert this to a JSON string, and pass it to our template, which will use JavaScript to display the data as markers on our map.

Getting data from SQL

We'll start in our `DBHelper` class—adding a method to return the fields we need for each crime in our database. Add the following method to your `dbhelper.py` file:

```python
def get_all_crimes(self):
 connection = self.connect()
 try:
  query = "SELECT latitude, longitude, date, category,
   description FROM crimes;"
  with connection.cursor() as cursor:
   cursor.execute(query)
  named_crimes = []
```

```
   for crime in cursor:
    named_crime = {
      'latitude': crime[0],
      'longitude': crime[1],
      'date': datetime.datetime.strftime(crime[2], '%Y-
        %m-%d'),
      'category': crime[3],
      'description': crime[4]
    }
    named_crimes.append(named_crime)
  return named_crimes
finally:
  connection.close()
```

Also, add the new `import` we need for the `datetime` module to the top of `dbhelper.py` via the following:

```
import datetime
```

We ignored the `id` and `updated_at` fields as the user is not interested in these using the SELECT operator to choose all our other fields. As we have no WHERE clause, this query will return all the crimes we have in our database. Once we have all the crimes, we could simply return them in their default representation of a tuple of tuples. However, this makes the maintenance of our application difficult. We don't want to have to remember that `latitude` is the first element of our tuple, `longitude` is the second, and so on. This would make developing the JavaScript part of our application a pain, as we'd have to keep referring back to our DBHelper to find out how exactly to grab, for example, just the `category` element of our data. If we wanted to make changes to our application in the future, it would probably require the same changes to be made here and in our JavaScript code.

Instead, we will create a dictionary from each of our records and return the dictionaries. This has two advantages: firstly, it's much easier to develop as we can refer to the elements of our data by name instead of by index, and secondly, we can easily convert our dictionary to JSON to be used in our JavaScript code. For most of the items in our dictionary, we will simply use the database column name as a key and the data itself as the value. The exception is the date; our database driver returns this as a Python `datetime` object, but we want to display it as a string for our user, so we will format it as "yyyy-mm-dd" before storing it in our dictionary.

We can add a stub of this method to our `MockDBHelper` so that we can continue to run our code locally without a database. In this case, instead of just returning a blank list, we'll return a mock crime, as well, in the same format that we'd expect from our real DBHelper. It's good practice to make any mock classes you create behave similarly to their real equivalents as this can help catch development errors while we're still testing locally.

Add the following function to `mockdbhelper.py`:

```
def get_all_crimes(self):
 return [{ 'latitude': -33.301304,
    'longitude': 26.523355,
    'date': "2000-01-01",
    'category': "mugging",
    'description': "mock description" }]
```

Passing the data to our template

Now that we have the ability to retrieve the data we want from our database by calling a single function, let's look at how we will use it in our main Flask app and pass it on to our template file.

Every time a user visits our home page, we want to get the crime data from the database and pass it to the template in JSON format to be displayed using JavaScript in our user's browser. As most of the hard work is done in our `DBHelper` class, we can keep our `home()` function quite neat. The entire function looks as follows:

```
@app.route("/")
def home():
 crimes = DB.get_all_crimes()
 crimes = json.dumps(crimes)
 return render_template("home.html", crimes=crimes)
```

We will use the `json.dumps()` function, which is the opposite of `json.loads()` that we used in the first project to create a JSON string for our dictionary (the letter "s" in `dumps` stands for "string") and then pass the JSON string on to our template so that it can use it to populate the map.

We also need to add an import for the JSON library. Near the top of `crimemap.py`, add the following line:

```
import json
```

Using the data in our template

Our template now has access to a JSON-formatted list of all the crimes in our database, and we can use this list to display markers on the map—one for each existing crime. We want to use the location data to choose where to place the marker, and then we want to embed `category`, `date`, and `description` as a label for our marker. This means that when the user moves his or her mouse over one of the markers, the information about the crime represented by this marker will be displayed.

We need to add a new function to our JavaScript code in our `home.html` file.
Under the `initialize()` function, add the following:

```
function placeCrimes(crimes) {
  for (i=0; i<crimes.length; i++) {
    crime = new google.maps.Marker( {
      position: new google.maps.LatLng(crimes[i].latitude, crimes[i].
longitude),
      map: map,
      title: crimes[i].date + "\n" +
       crimes[i].category + "\n" + crimes[i].description
      }
    );
  }
}
```

This function takes `crimes` an argument, loops through it, and creates a new marker
on our map (which we can refer to now as we previously made it a global variable)
for each crime in the list. We used the call to `google.maps.Marker()` to create the
marker and pass in a dictionary of arguments (in this case, a `google.maps.LatLng()`
"position", which we construct from our `latitude` and `longitude` parameters); a
reference to our map, which is `map`; and a concatenation of our `date`, `category`, and
`description`, separated by new line characters as the `title`.

> **Customizing Google Map markers**
>
> The marker we placed can be customized pretty heavily. The full list
> of options we can pass in can be seen at `https://developers.`
> `google.com/maps/documentation/javascript/`
> `reference?hl=en#MarkerOptions`.

All that's left is to make a call to our new function inside our `initialize()` function
and pass in the JSON map list that we built in Python. The entire `initialize()`
function is shown here with the new section highlighted:

```
function initialize() {
  var mapOptions = {
    center: new google.maps.LatLng(-33.30578381949298,
    26.523442268371582),
    zoom: 15
  };
  map = new google.maps.Map(document.getElementById("map-
    canvas"), mapOptions);
```

```
google.maps.event.addListener(map, 'click', function(event){
  placeMarker(event.latLng);
});
placeCrimes({{crimes | safe}});
}
```

We simply called our `placeCrimes()` function and passed in the crimes. Note that we used the Jinja built-in `safe` function by using the | (pipe) symbol and passing in our `crimes` data. This is necessary as, by default, Jinja escapes most special characters, but we need our JSON string to be interpreted raw with all special characters as is.

However, by using the `safe` function, we tell Jinja that we know that our data is safe and at this stage, this is not necessarily the case. Just because we have no malicious intent, it does not mean that all our data is inherently safe. Remember, most of the pieces of data were submitted by our users, and our data is therefore definitely not safe. We'll take a look at the big security hole we've opened in our app right after we make sure that it works (with normal, expected usage) as intended.

 If you're familiar with *nix shells, | or pipe should be pretty straightforward syntax. If not, think of it as a usual function with input and output. Instead of passing input as parameters in parentheses and using some form of a `return` function to get output, we will instead have our input on the left-hand side of the | symbol and the function name on the right-hand side (in this case, `safe`). The input gets piped through the function, and we are left with the output in place. This syntax can be very useful to chain lots of functions together, as each outer function is simply placed on the right-hand side after another | symbol.

Viewing the results

First, test out the code locally. This will make sure that everything still runs and will possibly catch some more subtle bugs as well. As we are using a mock for our database function, we won't have a lot of confidence that this works until we see it run on the VPS.

Once you run `python crimemap.py` in your terminal and visit `localhost:5000` in your browser, you should see the following:

We can note a single marker with the details we specified in our `MockDBHelper`. In the screenshot, we moved our mouse over the marker to make the `title` appear with all the details of the crime.

Now it's time to `commit` to `git` and push to our VPS. Run the following commands locally from your `crimemap` directory:

```
git add crimemap.py
git add dbhelper.py
git add mockdbhelper.py
git add templates/home.html
git commit -m "add new crimes functionality"
git push origin master
```

Then, SSH to your VPS to pull the new changes:

```
ssh username@123.456.789.123
cd /var/www/crimemap
git pull origin master
sudo service apache2 reload
```

If we visit the IP address of our VPS now, we should see the two crimes we added before we were able to display them. As we used the real DBHelper and our MySQL database for the production site, we should be able to add crimes using the form and see each crime added as a marker to the map in real time. Hopefully, you'll get something similar to the following screenshot:

If things don't work out as expected, as always run the following on your VPS and take a look at the output while visiting the site:

```
tail -f /var/log/apache2/error.log
```

Also, use your browser's debugger by pressing *Ctrl* + *Shift* + *C* to catch any JavaScript errors that might have crept in.

Our crime map is now functional and can already be used to start tracking crime in a town and keep people informed. However, we'll still add some finishing touches in the next chapter before moving on to our final project.

Summary

In this chapter, we looked at how to create a mock database in Python so that we could develop our application without needing access to a real database. We also added a Google Maps widget to our application and allowed our users to easily submit a latitude and longitude by clicking on the map while being able to view the locations and descriptions of existing crimes as well.

In the next chapter, we'll look at another injection vulnerability, XSS, and talk about how to protect against it as well as input validation in general.

8
Validating User Input in Our Crime Map Project

Users will always use your application in ways you didn't intend or expect, either out of ignorance or malicious intent. Every bit of input that the user has any control over should be validated to make sure it conforms to what is expected.

We'll polish off our second project by making sure that users can't break it accidentally or through maliciously crafted input.

In this chapter, we will cover the following topics:

- Choosing where to validate
- Trying out an XSS example
- Validating and sanitizing

Choosing where to validate

There are a few choices to make when it comes to validating user input and displaying feedback that helps them fix any mistakes they make. The major choice is *where* to do the validation: in the browser, on the server, or both.

We could do it in JavaScript in the user's browser. The advantages of this approach are that the users will get faster feedback (they don't have to wait to send data to our server, have it validated, and have a response sent back), and it also lightens the load on our server; if we don't use CPU cycles and network bandwidth to validate user data, it means we have lower costs associated with running our server. The disadvantage of this approach is that we have no assurance that the user will not bypass these checks; if the checks are run in the user's browser, then the user has full control over them. This means that data that is validated by client-side checks is still not guaranteed to be what we expect.

We could do it on the server after the user submits the data. The advantages and disadvantages of this approach are the opposite of those described earlier. We use more processing time that we're paying for, but we get extra assurance about the integrity of our checks. On the other hand, the user normally has to wait longer to get feedback about legitimate (not malicious) errors.

The final option is to do both. This gives us the best of all worlds; we can give fast feedback to the user in JavaScript, but then recheck the results on the server side to make sure that nothing got past our client-side checks. The flipside of this is that we end up wasting time on CPU cycles checking legitimate data twice, and we also have to put more effort into development as we have to write validation checks in JavaScript and in Python.

In this project, as we will implement our form management from scratch, we'll just do some very basic checks on the server side and no checking on the client side. In our next project, when we use frameworks to handle user input, we'll discuss how to easily use some more sophisticated validation methods.

Identifying inputs that require validation

We have already noted that not all browsers support the HTML5 `"date"` type input. This means that, as our site stands, some users will possibly type the date of the crime in manually, and this means that we need to be able to deal with the user inputting dates in various formats. Our database expects yyyy-mm-dd (for example, 2015-10-10 for October 10, 2015), but our users will not necessarily conform to this format even if we tell them to. The **Date** field, then, is one of the inputs we would want to validate.

Our **Latitude** and **Longitude** fields are also editable by the user, and therefore the user could enter text or other invalid coordinates in them. We could add validation checks for these, but, as the user should never actually need to edit these values, we'll instead consider how to make them *read only*. We'll add a validation check to make sure that the user has not left them blank, though.

The **Description** is the most obviously dangerous field. The user can freely input text here, and this means that the user has opportunities to *inject* code into our app. This means that instead of filling in a text description, as we'd probably expect, the user can input JavaScript or HTML code here that interferes with the code that we expect to run. Doing so would be an example of a so-called XSS or cross-site scripting attack, and we'll look at some malicious inputs that a user might use here.

Our last input is the **Category**. This might seem perfectly safe as the user has to select it from a drop-down list. However, it's important that the drop-down is merely a convenience, and, actually, a user with some very basic knowledge can use free-form text here as well. This is because the browser uses the information from the form to create a POST request, which it sends to our server. As a POST request is just text that is structured in a certain way and sent over HTTP; there is nothing stopping our tech-savvy users from constructing the POST request without using a web browser (they could use Python or another programming language instead or even some more specialized, but freely available software, such as BURP Suite).

As we can see, all of our inputs need validation in some form or another. Before we take a look at exactly how to go about validating input, let's take a brief look at what a malicious user might do if we decided not to implement validation.

Trying out an XSS example

One of the most sought-after attacks by malicious users is a so-called *persistent* XSS attack. This means that the attacker not only manages to inject code into your web app but this injected code also remains for an extended period of time. Most often, this is achieved by tricking the app into storing the malicious, injected code in a database and then running the code on a page on subsequent visits.

 In the following examples, we will *break* our application, specific inputs to our form. You will need to log in to the database on VPS afterwards to manually clear these inputs that leave our app in a broken state.

As our app currently stands, an attacker could carry out a persistent XSS attack by filing out the **Category**, **Date**, **Latitude**, and **Longitude** fields as usual, and using the following for the **Description** field:

```
</script><script>alert(1);</script>
```

This might look a bit strange, but give it a go. You should see the following:

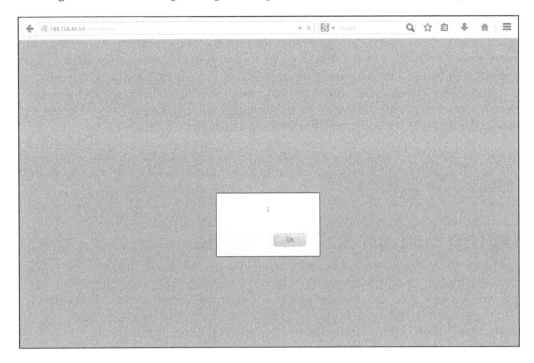

And after you click **OK** on the popup, you'll probably notice a strange excerpt from JavaScript at the top of our page (your value for `longitude` will be different, depending on where you placed the marker):

```
", "longitude": 26.52799}]); } function placeCrimes(crimes) { for
    (i=0; i
```

Let's look at what happened here. If we look at the full source code of our page, as it got interpreted by our browser, things will make more sense. Right-click on the page and click on **View Page Source** or an equivalent.

The `placecrimes()` call in the `initialize` function of our JavaScript code can be seen to now read as follows:

```
placeCrimes([{"latitude": -33.305645, "date": "2015-10-10",
"category": "mugging", "description":
"</script><script>alert(1);</script>", "longitude": 26.52799}]);
```

If your browser uses any form of code highlighting, it'll be easier to see what's happening. The opening `<script>` tag near the beginning of our page is now closed by the description of our first crime, as our browser knows to interpret anything that comes between `<script>` and `</script>` as JavaScript code. As we have `</script>` at the beginning of our `"description"`, the browser closes this section of JavaScript. Immediately after this, a new JavaScript section is opened by `<script>`, which is the next part of our description. Following this, we have `alert(1);`, which simply creates the pop-up box with **1** in it that we noted earlier. This script section is closed again, and the rest of our page is now interpreted as a mess by our browser. We can see the rest of our JSON (`"longitude": ...`) until halfway through our `for` loop is displayed to the user, and the `"<"` symbol from `i<crimes.length` is now interpreted by the browser as another opening tag so that the JavaScript that follows this is hidden again.

To fix our app, wipe all the crime data from your database with the following commands (which you should run on VPS):

```
mysql crimemap -p
<your database password>
delete from crimes;
```

You should see a message about how many crime records were deleted from the `crimes` table, similar to that seen in the following screenshot:

```
mysql> delete from crimes;
Query OK, 3 rows affected (0.02 sec)

mysql>
```

The potential of persistent XSS

It may seem pretty bad that our web application is broken. Worse still, reloading the page is not a solution. As the malicious description is stored in our database, the same issue will appear no matter how many times we reload the page. Even worse, the `"alert(1);"` example is just this—an example to show that the attacker has the freedom to run any code he or she desires. Often, an attacker uses this to trick the user into visiting another (malicious) page, banking on the fact that the user trusts the original page and will, therefore, be more likely trust the content on it. The possibilities are really only limited by our attacker's imagination.

Validating and sanitizing

To prevent the preceding, we've already chosen to inspect the data on the server side and make sure it conforms to our expectation. We still have a few more choices to make, though.

White and blacklisting

We need to create some rules to choose between acceptable inputs and unacceptable inputs, and there are two main ways of doing this. One way is to *blacklist* inputs that look malicious. Using this method, we would create a list of characters that might be used maliciously, such as "<" and ">", and we will reject inputs that contain these characters. The alternative is to use a *whitelist* approach. This is the opposite of blacklisting, in that, instead of choosing which characters we won't allow, we can choose a list of characters that we *will* allow.

It may seem like a nit-picky distinction, but it is important nonetheless. If we go with a blacklist approach, we are more likely to be outsmarted by malicious users who manage to inject code using only characters that we haven't added to our ban list.

On the other hand, using a whitelist approach, we are more likely to frustrate users who want to use characters which we haven't thought to add to the whitelist.

As our app only requires a `"description"` input to be free-text and because our app is localized (in the examples we used, the app is specific to Grahamstown, South Africa, and therefore we will expect our users to only need normal Latin characters and not, for example, Chinese characters), we should be able to employ whitelisting without getting in the way of our users.

Validating versus sanitizing

Next, we have to decide what to do with invalid input. Do we reject it completely and ask the user to try again, or do we just strip away the invalid parts of the user input and keep the rest? Removing or modifying user input (for example, by adding escape characters) is referred to as *sanitizing* the input. The advantage of this approach is that the user is often oblivious to it; if he or she inadvertently includes a special character in the description of the crime and we remove it, it's unlikely to make the rest of the description incomprehensible or worthless. The disadvantage is that if the user does end up relying on too many characters that we have blacklisted, it can corrupt the information to the point of being unusable or even misconstruing what the user intended.

Implementing validation

With all of the preceding in mind, we want to:

- Check the category that the user submits and make sure it is in the list of categories that we expect

- Check the date that the user submits and make sure that we can properly understand it as a date

- Check the latitude and longitude that the user submits and make sure that these are parsable as floating point numbers

- Check the description that the user submits and strip out all characters except for those that are alphanumeric or part of a preselected list of basic punctuation characters

Although we'll silently edit the description to remove non-whitelisted characters, we want to reject the entire submission and make the user start again if the other fields aren't as we expect. We, therefore, also want to add a way of displaying custom error messages to the user after he or she submits the form. Let's add a few Python functions to help us with all of this. We'll also restructure some of our code to conform to the *Don't repeat yourself(DRY)* principle.

Validating the category

Previously, when we created the drop-down list for categories, we hardcoded the two categories we wanted into our template. This is already not ideal as it means that we have to write our more boilerplate code (such as HTML tags) if we ever want to add or edit the categories. Now that we also want access the list of categories in Python, so that we can validate that the user hasn't sneakily used a category that isn't in our list, it makes sense to restructure it a bit so that we only define our list of categories once.

We'll define the list in our Python code and then we can pass it to our template to construct the drop-down list and use the same list for validation when the user submits the form. At the top of crimemap.py, along with our other globals, add the following:

```
categories = ['mugging', 'break-in']
```

In the return statement of the home() function, pass in this list as a named argument. The line should now look similar to this:

```
return render_template("home.html", crimes=crimes,
categories=categories)
```

In `home.html`, change the `<select>` block to use a Jinja `for` loop, as follows:

```
<select name="category" id="category">
    {% for category in categories %}
        <option value="{{category}}">{{category}}</option>
    {% endfor %}
</select>
```

With these small modifications, we have a much easier way to maintain our list of `categories`. We can now also use the new list to validate. As the category is provided by a drop-down list, the average user does not enter an invalid value here, so we don't have to worry too much about providing polite feedback. In this case, we'll just ignore the submission and return to the home page again.

Add the following `if` statement directly below where we loaded the category data into a variable in the `submitcrime()` function:

```
category = request.form.get("category")
if category not in categories:
    return home()
```

If triggered, this `return` would happen before we add anything to the database, and our user's attempted input would be discarded.

Validating the location

As our location data should be populated automatically by the marker that the user places on the map, we want to make these fields `readonly`. This means that our JavaScript will still be able to modify the values as the marker gets used, but the fields will reject input or modification from the user's keyboard. To do this, simply add the `readonly` attribute where we define the form in our `home.html` template. The updated `input` definitions should look as follows:

```
<label for="latitude">Latitude</label>
<input name="latitude" id="latitude" type="text" readonly>
<label for="longitude">Longitude</label>
<input name="longitude" id="longitude" type="text" readonly>
```

As with the drop-down list, though, the `readonly` property is only enforced at a browser level and is easily bypassed. We, therefore, want to add a server-side check as well. To do this, we'll use the Python philosophy of "it is better to ask for forgiveness than permission", or, in other words, assume everything will be OK and deal with the other cases in an `except` block instead of using too many `if` statements.

If we can parse the user's location data into floating point numbers, it's almost definitely safe as it's pretty difficult to do things such as modifying HTML, JavaScript, or SQL code using only numbers. Add the following code around the section of the `submitcrime()` function where we parse the location inputs:

```
try:
    latitude = float(request.form.get("latitude"))
    longitude = float(request.form.get("longitude"))
except ValueError:
    return home()
```

If there's any unexpected text in the `latitude` or `longitude` inputs, `ValueError` will be thrown when we attempt to cast to the float type, and, again, we'll return to the home page before putting any of the potentially dangerous data into our database.

Validating the date

For the `date` input, we could take the same approach as we did for the `category`. Most of the time, the user will select the date from a calendar picker and, therefore, will be unable to input an invalid date. However, as not all browsers support the `date` input type, sometimes, normal users will type out the dates manually, and this may lead to accidental error.

Therefore, in this case, we don't only want to reject invalid input. We want to, as far as possible, work out what the user intended, and if we cannot, we want to display a message to the user to indicate what needs to be fixed.

To allow for a more flexible input, we'll use a Python module called `dateparser`. This module allows us to take even inconsistently formatted dates and convert them into accurate Python `datetime` objects. The first thing we need to do is install it through `pip`. Run the following command locally *and* on VPS:

```
pip install --user dateparser
```

If you haven't used it before, you might like to play around a bit with the possibilities. The following standalone script demonstrates some of the magic that `dateparser` provides:

```
import dateparser
print dateparser.parse("1-jan/15")
print dateparser.parse("1 week and 3 days ago")
print(dateparser.parse("3/4/15"))
```

All the preceding strings are correctly parsed into `datetime` objects, except, arguably, the last one, as `dateparser` uses the American format and interprets it to be March 4, 2015, instead of April 3, 2015.

Some more examples as well as other information about the dateparser module can be found on PyPI at https://pypi.python.org/pypi/dateparser.

Just using this package will solve a lot of our problems as we can now transform invalid inputs into valid ones without any help from the user at all. The slight inconvenience is that we have already set up our database to accept dates to be inserted as strings in the "*yyyy-mm-dd*" format; however, to take advantage of our new dateparser module, we'll want to convert the user's input to a datetime object. The slightly counterintuitive workaround is to convert the string input we receive from the user to a datetime object and then back to a string (which will always be in the correct format) before passing it into our database code to store in MySQL.

First off, add the following helper function to your crimemap.py file:

```
def format_date(userdate):
    date = dateparser.parse(userdate)
    try:
        return datetime.datetime.strftime(date, "%Y-%m-%d")
    except TypeError:
        return None
```

Also, add the imports for the datetime and dateparser modules to the top of crimemap.py, as follows:

```
import datetime
import dateparser
```

We'll pass the date as input by our user (userdate) into this function and parse this using our dateparser module. If the date is completely unparsable (for example, "aaaaa"), the dateparser.parse function will just return nothing instead of throwing an error. Therefore, we will put the call to strftime, which will format the date as a string in the correct format into a try except block; if our date variable is empty, we'll get a TypeError, in which case our helper function will also return None.

Now, we need to decide what to do in case we cannot parse the date. Unlike the other validation cases we looked at, in this case, we want to prompt the user with a message saying that we were unable to understand his or her input. To achieve this, we'll add an error message parameter to the home() function and pass in a relevant error message from the submitcrime() function. Modify the home() function to add the parameter and to pass the parameter into our template, as follows:

```
@app.route("/")
def home(error_message=None):
    crimes = DB.get_all_crimes()
    crimes = json.dumps(crimes)
    return render_template("home.html", crimes=crimes,
categories=categories, error_message=error_message)
```

Then, modify the `submitcrime()` function to add some logic to parsing the date input by our user and to pass an error message to our `home()` function if we fail to parse the `date`, as follows:

```
if category not in categories:
    return home()
date = format_date(request.form.get("date"))
if not date:
    return home("Invalid date. Please use yyyy-mm-dd format")
```

We also need to add a section to our template file to display the error message if it exists. We'll add it to the top of the form where it should catch the user's attention via the following code:

```
<div id="newcrimeform">
    <h2>Submit new crime</h2>
    {% if error_message %}
        <div id="error"><p>{{error_message}}</p></div>
    {% endif %}
    <form action="/submitcrime" method="POST">
```

We will add the preceding `if` statement as we'll otherwise see the word "None" appear above our form when the `error_message` variable has its default value of None. Also, note that the message itself appears in a `<div>` tag with an ID of error. This allows us to add some CSS to make the error message appear in red. Add the following block to your `style.css` file in your static directory:

```
#error {
    color: red;
}
```

That's it for validating our date. If you have a browser that does not support the `date` input, try creating a new crime and inputting a string that even `dateparser` cannot interpret as a legitimate date to make sure you see the error as expected. It should look something similar to the following image:

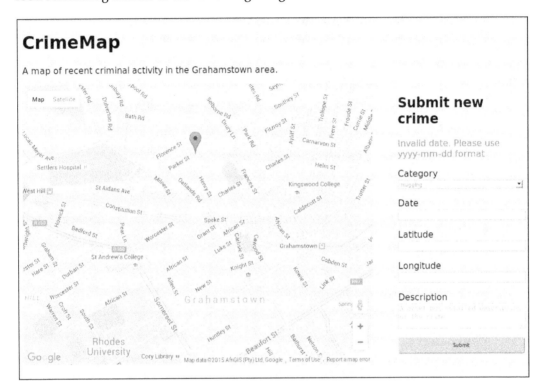

 Flask provides some pretty nifty functionality for message *flashing* — that is, to display optional text to the user at a specific position on the page. This has some more powerful and flexible functionality than the basic example we discussed, and should certainly be considered for similar cases. Information about message flashing in Flask can be found at `http://flask.pocoo.org/docs/0.10/patterns/flashing/`.

Validating the description

We can assume that a user will be able to convey basic information about a crime using only numbers, letters (capital and lowercase), and some basic punctuation marks, so let's create a simple Python function that filters out all characters from a string except the ones we have identified as safe. Add the following `sanitize()` function to your `crimemap.py` file:

```
def sanitize_string(userinput):
    whitelist = string.letters + string.digits + " !?$.,;:-'()&"
    return filter(lambda x: x in whitelist, userinput)
```

Then, add the import for string to the imports section of `crimemap.py`, as follows:

```
import string
```

Our `sanitize_string()` function is quite concise, and uses some of Python's functional programming potential. The `filter` function applies another function repeatedly for each element in a list and builds a new list based on the ones that "pass." In this case, the function that we will pass into `filter()` is a simple `lambda` function that checks whether or not a letter belongs to our `whitelist`. The result of our function is a string similar to the input one, but with all the characters that aren't part of our whitelist removed.

Our whitelist is built from all the letters (uppercase and lowercase), the digits one to nine, and some basic punctuation marks that people may use while typing informal descriptions of events.

To use our new function, simply change the line near the end of the `submitcrime()` function in `crimemap.py` from the following to the subsequent:

```
description = request.form.get("description")
description = sanitize_string(request.form.get("description"))
```

Note that, as our SQL driver mitigates against SQL injection and our `json.dumps()` function escapes double quotation marks, we should be largely safe just by blacklisting characters such as angle brackets, which we used to demonstrate an XSS attack. This would allow more flexibility for our users, but malicious users can be determined and creative in crafting input that will bypass the filters we set up. Refer to `https://www.owasp.org/index.php/XSS_Filter_Evasion_Cheat_Sheet` for some examples. Give the validation changes a go locally first and then, if everything looks good by committing to `git`, push the repo to the remote, and pull it onto VPS. Restart Apache and visit your IP address. Try submitting a crime using `</script>` in the `description`, and you'll notice when you hover the cursor over the marker for this crime that all we've stored is "script". We will strip the slash and the angle brackets, thus ensuring protection against XSS.

We already discussed the pros and cons of blacklisting and whitelisting, but, to emphasise that whitelisting is not a perfect approach, take a look at the post here about mistakes developers often make when whitelisting an input for users' names: `http://www.kalzumeus.com/2010/06/17/falsehoods-programmers-believe-about-names/`

The last change we can make to our dbhelper.py, mockdbhelper.py, and crimemap. py files is to remove the functions we no longer need. When we had a basic database application that was not specific to crimes, we had the get_all_inputs(), add_ input(), and clear_all() functions in our DBHelper classes and the add() and clear() functions in our crimemap.py file. All of these can be removed.

Summary

We have spent a whole chapter looking at validation, but if you look at the major companies that have faced information security breaches over the last few years, you'll agree that security is worth spending some time on. We looked specifically at cross-site scripting or XSS attacks, but we also discussed some more general points of input validation. This takes us to the end of our second project.

One thing that is notably missing is to work out who added which crimes. If one malicious user adds a bunch of bogus crimes to our database, they could potentially mess up our entire dataset!

In our next project, we'll look at authenticating users through a User Account Control system, which will give us more control over who we let on our site and what they can do.

Building a Waiter Caller App

9

After going through the headlines project, in which you learned the basics of Flask, and the Crimemap project, in which you learned about some more useful Flask features, such as how to use a database and how to write some basic JavaScript code, we're now ready for our most sophisticated project yet! We will build a waiter caller web application that allows restaurant patrons to easily call a waiter to their table. The restaurant manager will easily be able to register for and start using our application without the need to invest in expensive hardware.

We will dive even deeper into the Flask world, taking a look at some Flask extensions to help us with user account control and web forms, and we'll look at how to use template inheritance in Jinja, too. We'll also use the Bootstrap frontend framework so that we don't have to do so much of the HTML and CSS code from scratch.

In contrast with the MySQL database we used for our previous application, we'll take a look at a controversial alternative: MongoDB. MongoDB is a NoSQL database, which means that we don't deal with tables, rows, and columns in it. We'll also discuss exactly what this means.

One of the most difficult tasks for a waiter is to know when a patron needs something. Either the patron complains that they waited for far too long before the waiter came and asked about dessert options, or they complain that the waiter was constantly interrupting conversation in order to ask whether everything was all right. In order to solve this problem, some restaurants install dedicated buttons at each table which, when pressed, notify the waiter that his attention is wanted. However, the cost of specialized hardware and installation is prohibitive for smaller establishments and often just too much hassle for larger ones.

In our modern day and age, nearly all restaurant-goers have smartphones, and we can leverage this fact to provide restaurants with a much more cost-effective solution. When patrons want attention, they will simply visit a short URL on their phone, and the waiters will receive a notification on a centralized screen.

We want the application to allow for multiple, unrelated restaurants to use the same web application, so each should have a private login account for our system. We want it to be easy for the restaurant manager to set up; that is, we as developers should not need to be involved at all when a new restaurant joins the system.

The setup required for our application is as follows:

- The restaurant manager signs up a new account on our web application
- The restaurant manager provides basic information about how many tables the restaurant has
- The web application provides a unique URL for each table
- The restaurant manager prints out these URLs and ensures that the relevant URL is easily accessible from each table

The usage of our application should have the following features:

- The restaurant staff should be able to log into the web application from a centralized screen and see a simple notification page.
- Some patrons would want service and visit the URL relevant to their table on a smartphone, so this should be possible.
- In real time, the waiters should see a notification appear on a centralized screen. The waiter will then acknowledge the notification on the screen and attend to the patrons.
- If more notifications arrive before the first one is acknowledged, the later ones should appear beneath the earlier ones.

Over the next three chapters, we'll implement a Flask application that has all of the preceding features. We'll have a database to store the account information of all the individual restaurants that register to use our application so that we can process patron requests for each of them individually. Patrons will be able to make requests, which will be registered in the database, while the restaurant staff will be able to view current attention requests for their establishment. We'll build a user account control system so that restaurants can have their own password-protected accounts for our application.

To start with, we'll set up a new Flask application, Git repository, and Apache configuration to serve our new project. We'll introduce Twitter's Bootstrap framework as the one we'll use on the frontend. We'll download a basic Bootstrap template as a start for the frontend of our application and make some changes to integrate it into a basic Flask application. Then, we'll set up a user account control system that allows users to register, log in, and log out of our application by supplying an e-mail address and password.

In this chapter, we'll cover the following topics:

- Setting up a new git repository
- Using Bootstrap to kick-start our application
- Adding User Account Control to our application

Setting up a new Git repository

As before, we need to create a new git repository to host our new project. The first step is to go to log into the web interface of BitBucket or whichever code repository host you are using, select the **Create a new Repository** option, and select the **Git** radio option, taking note of the URL with which it provides you. As the next steps are identical to the previous projects, we will give you only a summary. If you need more fine-grained guidance, refer to the *Installing and using git* section of *Chapter 1, Hello, World!*.

Setting up the new project locally

To set up the local project structure, run the following commands locally:

```
mkdir waitercaller
cd waitercaller
git init
git remote add origin <new-repository-url>
mkdir templates
mkdir static
touch waitercaller.py
touch templates/home.html
touch .gitignore
```

We want to get the minimal running app for this project so that we can iron out any configuration issues before we get started with development. Add the following to your waitercaller.py file:

```
from flask import Flask

app = Flask(__name__)

@app.route("/")
def home():
    return "Under construction"

if __name__ == '__main__':
    app.run(port=5000, debug=True)
```

Then, push the project outline to the repository with the following commands:

```
git add .
git commit -m "Initial commit"
git push origin master
```

Setting up the project on our VPS

On your VPS, run the following commands to clone the repository, and set up Apache2 to serve our new project as the default website:

```
cd /var/www/
git clone <new-repository-url>
cd waitercaller
nano waitercaller.wsgi
```

Add the following code to the .wsgi file we created with the most recent command:

```
import sys
sys.path.insert(0, "/var/www/waitercaller")
from waitercaller import app as application
```

Now, hit *Ctrl* + *X* and select *Y* when prompted to quit Nano.

Lastly, create the Apache configuration file by running the following:

```
cd /etc/apache2/sites-available
nano waitercaller.conf
```

Add the following configuration data to the `waitercaller.conf` file we just created:

```
<VirtualHost *>

    WSGIScriptAlias / /var/www/waitercaller/waitercaller.wsgi
    WSGIDaemonProcess waitercaller
    <Directory /var/www/waitercaller>
        WSGIProcessGroup waitercaller
        WSGIApplicationGroup %{GLOBAL}
         Order deny,allow
         Allow from all
    </Directory>
</VirtualHost>
```

Quit Nano, saving the new file as before. Now, to disable our `crimemap` project as the default site and enable our new project instead, run the following commands:

```
sudo a2dissite crimemap.conf
sudo a2ensite waitercaller.conf
sudo service apache2 reload
```

Verify that everything worked by visiting the IP address of your VPS in your web browser. You should see the **Under construction** string. Have another look at your configuration and log files if things don't work out as expected.

Using Bootstrap to kick-start our application

In our previous projects, we spent quite a bit of time on frontend work, fiddling around with CSS and HTML, and we didn't even touch on some of the frontend problems that web application developers need to be aware of, such as making sure our content looks good and functions correctly on all devices of all screen sizes running any browser on any operating system. This diversity of browsers and devices as well as the inconsistent way in which each of them implements certain JavaScript, HTML, and CSS functionality is one of the biggest challenges of web development, and there is no silver bullet to solve the problem. However, frontend frameworks such as Bootstrap can take away some of the pain, providing shortcuts for developers to improve their user experience.

Introducing Bootstrap

Bootstrap was developed by Twitter and is released under an open license. It can greatly speed up CSS development as it provides many styles for different HTML layouts and form inputs. It can also provide *responsiveness*; that is, it can allow your website to automatically change the layout of certain elements based on the screen size of your user's device. We'll discuss exactly what this means for us and for this project later in the chapter.

Bootstrap has faced some criticism, but it still holds its popularity. There are many alternatives with different strengths and weaknesses. As modern web development is a fast-evolving field, there are also many new frameworks that appear regularly. Existing frameworks often get major updates and don't provide backward compatibility to old versions. For important production web applications, current research into what best fits the specific needs of this project is always crucial.

Bootstrap's main offerings are reusable in CSS and JavaScript modules. We'll mainly use it for its CSS components.

Take a look at Bootstrap's homepage at `http://getbootstrap.com/` as well as the subpages at `http://getbootstrap.com/getting-started/#examples` and `http://getbootstrap.com/components/` to get an idea of what Bootstrap provides.

Instead of writing CSS from scratch, Bootstrap allows us to use various inputs, icons, navigation bars, and other often-needed components of a website that look good by default.

Downloading Bootstrap

There are a few ways to install Bootstrap, but keeping in mind that Bootstrap can be thought of as a collection of some JavaScript, CSS, and icon files, we will not do anything too fancy. We can simply download a `.zip` file of the compiled code files and use these files in our local project. We'll include bootstrap in our `git` repository, so there is no need to install it on our VPS as well. Perform the following steps:

1. Head over to `http://getbootstrap.com/getting-started/#download` and select the **Download Bootstrap** option, which should be the compiled and minified version without documentation.

2. Unzip the file you downloaded, and you'll find a single directory called `bootstrap-3.x.x` (here, the repeated letter x represents numbers that indicate which version of Bootstrap is contained). Inside the directory, there will be some subdirectories, probably `js`, `css`, and `fonts`.

3. Copy the `js`, `css`, and `fonts` directories to the `static` directory of the `waitercaller` project. Your project should now have the following structure:

```
waitercaller/
templates
    home.html
static
    css/
    fonts/
    js
.gitignore
waitercaller.py
```

Because of the regular Bootstrap updates, we included a complete copy of the code for Bootstrap 3.3.5 in the accompanying code bundle (the latest version during the writing of this book). While the latest version is probably better, it might not be compatible with the examples we give. You can choose to test the waters with the version we provide, knowing that the examples should work as expected, or jump in at the deep end and, if necessary, try to work out how to adapt the examples to the newer Bootstrap code.

Bootstrap templates

Bootstrap strongly encourages users to build customized frontend pages instead of simply using existing templates. You've probably noticed a lot of modern web pages look very similar; this is because frontend designing is difficult, and people like taking shortcuts. As this book focuses on Flask development, we'll also take a bit of a frontend shortcut and start with one of the example template files that Bootstrap provides. The template file we'll work with can be seen at `http://getbootstrap.com/examples/jumbotron/`, and the adaptation for our project can be found in the accompanying code bundle for this chapter at `tempates/home.html`. You can note from the similarity of the two files that we didn't have to do too much work to get a basic web page that also looks good.

Copy the code from the `templates/home.html` file in the code bundle to the same place in your own project directory that we created earlier. If you included all the Bootstrap files properly in your `static` folder, opening this new file directly in your web browser will result in a page that looks similar to the following screenshot. (Note that at this stage, we still use pure HTML and none of the Jinja functionality, so you can just open the file locally in your web browser instead of serving it from a Flask application.):

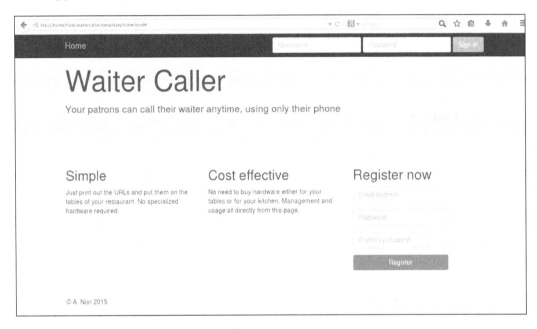

We can note the advantages of the styling of inputs, headers, the navigation bar, and Jumbotron (the gray bar near the top with the oversized **Waiter Caller** text in it) that we can achieve with very little code. However, perhaps the most significant time-saving element of using Bootstrap is the *responsiveness* that our site has. Bootstrap is based on a grid layout, which means that different elements of the grid can rearrange themselves to better fit on any device. Note this part of HTML from the template:

```
<div class="row">
  <div class="col-md-4">
    <h2>Simple</h2>
```

A `"row"` has space for 12 columns. Our three main content elements below the Jumbotron each take up four columns, thus filling the row (*4 x 3 = 12*). We specified this using the `class="col-md-4"` attribute. Think of this as a medium (md) column of size four. You can read more about how the grid system works and take a look at some examples at `http://getbootstrap.com/css/`.

There's also some code that doesn't look used in the preceding screenshot, similar to this:

```
<button type="button" class="navbar-toggle collapsed" data-
    toggle="collapse" data-target="#navbar" aria-expanded="false"
    aria-controls="navbar">
```

The two preceding excerpts are perhaps the most important components in making our web application responsive. To understand what this means, resize your browser window while the page is open. This simulates how our page will be seen on smaller devices, such as phones and tablets. It should look similar to the following screenshot:

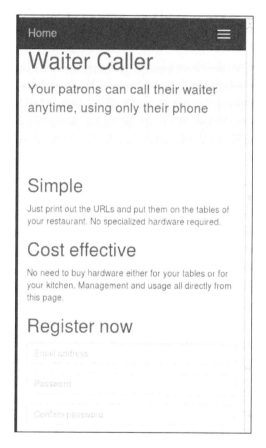

We can note that our three main content elements that used the Bootstrap grid functionality are now arranged beneath each other instead of side by side. This is ideal for smaller devices in which users are more used to scrolling down than to looking for more content on the side. Our navigation bar has also become more concise with the login inputs now hidden.

These can be revealed by selecting the *hamburger* icon in the upper right-hand corner; this is a controversial, but highly prevalent, element in web development. Most users instinctively know that they can touch the icon to get some form of menu or expansion, but there are many criticisms of using this technique. For now, we'll just accept this as normal practice and not go into the problems behind it. It's definitely better than trying to display exactly the same content no matter the screen size and having our users zoom into the page section by section, depending on which part they need to see.

Adding user account control to our application

For user account control, a user is expected to log in and authenticate using a password. For example, when you log in to your Webmail account, you enter your password upon visiting the page. Thereafter, all your actions are taken as authenticated; that is, you do not have to enter your password again when you send an e-mail. The Webmail client *remembers* that you are logged in, and you are therefore allowed to complete certain actions.

However, HTTP is a stateless protocol, which means that we have no direct way of knowing that the user who logged in is the same user who made the request to send an e-mail. As a workaround for this problem, we will give the user a cookie when he or she logs in initially, and the user's browser will then send this cookie to us with *every* subsequent request. We'll use our database to keep track of which users are currently logged in. This allows us to authenticate the user for every request without requesting the user's password multiple times.

We could implement this from scratch using Flask cookies in a similar way to what we saw in our Headlines project. However, there are numerous steps that we would need to implement, such as selecting which pages in our application require authentication and ensuring that the cookie is secure, and be involved in deciding what information to store in the cookie.

Instead, we'll go up one level of abstraction and use the `Flask-Login` extension.

Introducing Flask-Login

`Flask-Login` is a Flask extension that implements the groundwork required for all user account control systems. To use this, we need to install it through `pip` and then create a user class that follows a specific pattern. You can find a summary of `Flask-Login` as well as comprehensive documentation at `https://flask-login.readthedocs.org/en/latest/`.

Installing and importing Flask-Login

To install `Flask-Login`, run the following command:

```
pip install --user flask-login
```

As with all the Python modules we install, remember to do this both locally and on your VPS.

To begin with, we'll add the most basic login functionality possible. Our application will display **You are logged in** for users who have authenticated, but users who do not enter a correct password will not be able to see the message.

Using Flask extensions

When we install Flask extensions, we can automatically access them through the `flask.ext` path. The first class we'll use from the `Flask-Login` extension is the so-called `LoginManager` class. We'll also use the `@login_required` decorator to specify which routes are restricted to users who are logged in. Add the following imports to your `waitercaller.py` file:

```
from flask.ext.login import LoginManager
from flask.ext.login import login_required
```

Now, we need to connect the extension to our Flask app. In a pattern that will become familiar as we use more Flask extensions, add the following line to `waitercaller.py` directly below the place where you create the `app` variable:

```
app = Flask(__name__)
login_manager = LoginManager(app)
```

The `LoginManager` class we instantiated now has a reference to our application. We'll use this new `LoginManager` class to—you guessed it—manage logins for our application.

Adding a restricted route

Now, let's add a route to our application at `/account` and make sure that only authenticated users can view this page. The easy part of this step is to make sure that *non* authenticated users *can't* see the page, so we'll start with this.

First, we want our application to render our Bootstrap template by default. Add the following route to the `waitercaller.py` file:

```
@app.route("/")
def home():
    return render_template("home.html")
```

Now, we'll add a restricted route that users who aren't logged in can't see. Add the following function to `waitercaller.py`:

```
@app.route("/account")
@login_required
def account():
    return "You are logged in"
```

Note that we're using the `@login_required` decorator. Similarly to the `@app.route` decorator, this is a function that takes the function below it as input and returns a modified function. In this case, instead of the routing magic, it'll verify that the user is logged in, and if not, it'll redirect the user to an **Unauthorized** page instead of returning the content we specified in the `return` statement. It's important that the `@app.route` decorator is first and the `@login_required` one is below it, as in the preceding example.

> You've probably seen **404 page not found** errors sometimes while browsing the Web. While **404** is especially infamous, there are many error codes that are part of the HTTP specification. Different browsers may show different default error messages when these are received, and it's also possible to define custom error pages to be shown when the specified errors are hit.

As we haven't set up any of the login logic yet, no user should be able to authenticate and view the new route we created. Start your Flask application locally and try to visit the account route at `localhost:5000/account`. If all went well, you should see an unauthorized error message similar to the following screenshot:

Authenticating a user

The Internet can be a dark and scary place. This is why you need to put passwords into many web applications; the password proves that you are who you claim to be. By telling us something that only you know, the web application knows you are "you" and not an imposter.

The simplest way to implement a password checking system would be to store passwords associated with usernames in a database. When the user logs in, you need to first verify that the username exists, and if it does, you need to verify that the password the user just gave matches the one that he or she used when registering.

In practice, this is a terrible idea. Databases may be accessed by any number of people, including employees of the company that runs the web application and, potentially, hackers. Instead, we'll eventually store a cryptographic hash of the user's password; however for now, to make sure our login system works, we'll work with plaintext passwords.

We'll set up a mock database that is very similar to the one we used in our Crime Map project and check whether we can allow a mock user to view our account page if, and only if, the correct password is entered.

Creating a user class

As we are using the Flask-Login module, we need to create a User class that conforms to a strict format. Flask-Login is flexible enough to allow some more advanced login functionality, such as distinguishing between *active* and *nonactive* accounts as well as anonymous users. We won't use these features, but we need to create a User class that can work with Flask-Login, so we'll have some methods that look redundant.

Create a new file called user.py in your waitercaller directory. Add the following code to it:

```
class User:
    def __init__(self, email):
        self.email = email

    def get_id(self):
        return self.email

    def is_active(self):
        return True

    def is_anonymous(self):
        return False

    def is_authenticated(self):
        return True
```

Flask-Login requires that we implement a get_id() method in our User class that returns a unique identifier for the user. We'll be using the user's e-mail address for this, so in the get_id() function we can simply return that.

We'll regard all our users as having active accounts; so, in this method, which is also required, we'll simply return True. The opposite goes for the is_anonymous() function; while this is also required, we won't deal with the concept of anonymous logins in our application, so we'll always return False.

The last function may look a bit odd; we'll always return True for is_authenticated(). This is because we only create the user object when the correct username and password combination is entered, so if the user object exists, it'll be authenticated.

Mocking our database for users

We'll create a MockDBHelper class again and also create a configuration file to indicate that this should be used locally when we test our application and don't have access to the database. It needs to have a function that takes a username and password and checks whether these exist in the database and are associated with each other.

First, create a file called mockdbhelper.py in your waitercaller directory and add the following code:

```
MOCK_USERS = {'test@example.com': '123456'}

class MockDBHelper:

    def get_user(self, email):
        if email in MOCK_USERS:
            return MOCK_USERS[email]
        return None
```

At the top, we have a dictionary that acts as the database storage. We have a single get_user() method that checks whether a user exists in our database and returns the password if it does.

Now, create a config.py file in the waitercaller directory and add the single line as follows:

```
test = True
```

As in our last project, this file will let our application know whether it is running in our test (local) environment or in our production (VPS) one. Unlike our previous project, we'll add other information into this file later that doesn't involve the database, which is why we'll call it `config.py` instead of `dbconfig.py`. We don't want to check this file into our `git` repository as it'll be different on our VPS and will also contain sensitive database credentials that we don't want to store; so, create a `.gitignore` file in your `waitercaller` directory with the following lines:

```
config.py
*.pyc
```

Logging in a user

Our template already has a login form set up that allows a user to enter an e-mail and a password. We'll now set up functionality that allows us to enter and check the input into this form against our mock database. If we enter an e-mail and password that exist in our mock database, we'll log the user in and allow access to our `/account` route. If not, we'll just redirect back to the home page (we'll look at displaying feedback to a user who inputs invalid information in the next chapter in the *Adding user feedback using WTForms* section).

Adding imports and configuration

We need to import the `login_user` function that is part of the `Flask-Login` extension as well as our new `User` class code and database helper. Add the following lines to your imports in `waitercaller.py`:

```
from flask.ext.login import login_user

from mockdbhelper import MockDBHelper as DBHelper
from user import User
```

As we don't have a database helper except for our mock one at the moment, we'll always import the mock one. Later, we'll use the value in `config.py` to decide which database helper to `import` — the real or mock one — as we did in our previous project.

We also need to create a `DBHelper` global class so that our application code can easily talk to our database. Add the following line beneath the import section of `waitercaller.py`:

```
DB = DBHelper()
```

Finally, we also need to configure a secret key for our application. This is used to cryptographically sign the session information cookies that `Flask-Login` hands out to our users when they log in. Signing the cookies prevents our users from editing them manually, which helps prevent fraudulent logins. For this step, you should create a long and secure secret key; you will never have to remember it, so don't think about it as you would about a password or passphrase. Although randomly mashing your keyboard should be sufficient, humans are generally terrible at creating unbiased randomness, so you could also use the following command to create a random string using `/dev/urandom` (changing `100` to the number of characters you want) via the following:

```
cat /dev/urandom | base64 | head -c 100 ; echo
```

Once you have a long random string of characters, add the following line to your `waitercaller.py` file under the place where you declared the `app` variable, substituting the random characters for your own:

```
app.secret_key = 'tPXJY3X37Qybz4QykV+hOyUxVQeEXf1Ao2C8upz+fGQXKsM'
```

Adding the login functionality

There are two main parts of logging a user in to consider. The first is when the user enters an e-mail address and password to authenticate, and the second is when the user does so by sending the required cookie—that is, he or she is still in the same browser *session* as when a successful login was completed.

Writing the login function

We already created the stub of our login route for the first case, so now, we will flesh that out a bit to check the input information against our database and use `Flask-Login` to log the user in if the e-mail and password match.

We'll also introduce a cleaner way of calling one Flask route from a separate one. Add the following lines to the imports section of `waitercaller.py`:

```
from flask import redirect
from flask import url_for
```

The first takes a URL and creates a response for a route that simply redirects the user to the URL specified. The second builds a URL from a function name. In Flask applications, you'll often see these two functions used together, as in the following example.

Write the login function in `waitercaller.py` to match what follows through this code:

```
@app.route("/login", methods=["POST"])
def login():
    email = request.form.get("email")
    password = request.form.get("password")
    user_password = DB.get_user(email)
    if user_password and user_password == password:
        user = User(email)
        login_user(user)
        return redirect(url_for('account'))
    return home()
```

We also need to add `import` for the `request` library. Add the following line to the `import` section of `waitercaller.py`:

```
from flask import request
```

We'll load the user's input into `email` and `password` variables and then load the stored password into a `user_password` variable. The `if` statement is verbose as we explicitly verified that a password was returned (that is, we verified that the user exists) and that the password was correct, even though the second condition implies the first. Later on, we'll talk about the trade-off of differentiating between the two conditions when giving feedback to our user.

If everything is valid, we will create a `User` object from the e-mail address, now using the e-mail address as the unique identifier required by Flask login. We will then pass our `User` object to the `Flask-Login` module's `login_user()` function so that it can handle the authentication magic. If the login is successful, we will redirect the user to the account page. As the user is now logged in, this will return the `"You are logged in"` string instead of the `"Unauthorized"` error we got before.

Note that we will create a URL for our account page using the `url_for()` function. We will pass the result of this into the `redirect()` function so that the user is taken from the `/login` route to the `/account` one. This is preferable to simply using the following:

```
return account()
```

Our intention is more explicit, and the user will see the correct URL in the browser (that is, both will take the user to the `/account` page), but if we don't use the `redirect()` function, `/login` will still be displayed in the browser even on the `/account` page.

Creating the load_user function

If the user has already logged in, their browser will send us information through the cookie that `Flask-Login` gave them when we called the `login_user` function. This cookie contains a reference to the unique identifier we specified when we created our `User` object—in our case, the e-mail address.

`Flask-Login` has an existing function that we called `user_loader`, which will handle this for us; we just need to use it as a decorator for our own function that checks the database to make sure the user exists and creates a `User` object from the identifier we are given.

Add the following function to your `waitercaller.py` file:

```
@login_manager.user_loader
def load_user(user_id):
    user_password = DB.get_user(user_id)
    if user_password:
        return User(user_id)
```

The decorator indicates to `Flask-Login` that this is the function we want to use to handle users who already have a cookie assigned, and it'll pass the `user_id` variable from the cookie to this function whenever a user visits our site, which already has one. Similarly to what we did before, we will check whether the user is in our database (`user_password` will be blank if `user_id` is invalid), and if it is, we will recreate the `User` object. We'll never explicitly call this function or use the result as it'll only be used by the `Flask-Login` code, but our application will throw an error if a user who is given a cookie by our `login()` function visits the site and `Flask-Login` can't find an implementation for this `user_loader()` function.

It might seem unnecessary to check the database in this step considering we gave the user a supposedly tamper-proof token that proves that he or she is a valid user, but it is in fact necessary as the database may have been updated since the user last logged in. If we make the user's session token valid for a long time (recall that in our Headlines project, we made the cookies last for a year), there is the possibility that the user's account will have been modified or deleted since the cookie was assigned.

Checking the login functionality

It's time to give our new login functionality a try! Fire up the `waitercaller.py` file locally and visit `localhost:5000` in your web browser. Type in the e-mail ID `test@example.com` and password `123456` from our mock database and hit the login button. You should be redirected to `http://localhost:5000/account` and view the **You are logged in** message.

Close your browser and reopen it, this time visiting `localhost:5000/account` directly. As we didn't tell `Flask-Login` to remember users, you should now see the **Unauthorized** error again.

Because of the nature of our application, we would expect most users to want to stay logged in so that the restaurant staff can simply open the page in the morning and use the functionality straightaway. `Flask-Login` makes this change very straightforward. Simply change the line of your `login()` function that reads the following:

```
login_user(user)
```

Your new `login()` function should now read:

```
login_user(user, remember=True)
```

Now, if you repeat the preceding steps, you should view the **You are logged in** message as shown in the following screenshot, even after restarting your browser:

Now that we can log a user in, let's take a look at how we can allow the user to log out as well.

Logging out a user

`Flask-Login` provides a logout function that works straight out of the box. All we have to do is link it up to a route. Add the following route to your `waitercaller.py` file:

```
@app.route("/logout")
def logout():
    logout_user()
    return redirect(url_for("home"))
```

Then, add the `import` for the `logout_user()` function to the imports section of `waitercaller.py`:

```
from flask.ext.login import logout_user
```

Note here that there's no need to pass the `User` object to `Flask-Login` for this call; the `logout()` function simply removes the session cookie from the user's browser. Once the user is logged out, we can redirect them back to the home page.

Visit `localhost:5000/logout` in your browser and then attempt to visit `localhost:5000/account` again. You should see the **Unauthorized** error again as the `test@example.com` user got logged out.

Registering a user

It's great that we can log users in, but at the moment we can only do so with the mock user that we hardcoded into our database. We need to be able to add new users to our database when the registration form is filled out. We'll still do all of this through our mock database, so every time our application is restarted, all the users will be lost (they will only be saved in the local Python dictionary variable, which is lost when the application is terminated).

We mentioned that storing the users' passwords was a very bad idea; so first, we'll take a brief look at how cryptographic hashing works and how we can manage passwords more securely.

Managing passwords with cryptographic hashes

Instead of storing the password, we want to store something that is *derived from* the password. When the user registers and gives us a password, we'll run some modification on it and store the result of the modification instead. Then, the next time the user visits our site and uses the password to log in, we can run the same modification on the input password and verify that the result matches what we stored.

The catch is that we want our modification to be nonreversible; that is, someone who has access to the modified password should not be able to deduce the original.

Enter hash functions. These little pieces of mathematical wizardry take a string as input and return a (big) number as output. The same string input will always result in the same output, but it is almost impossible for two different inputs to produce the same output. Hash functions are so-called *one-way* functions as it is provably impossible to deduce the input if you only have the output.

Password storage and management is a big topic that we can only touch on in this project. For more information on most things regarding information security, www.owasp.org is a good resource. Their comprehensive guide to storing passwords securely can be found at https://www.owasp.org/index.php/Password_Storage_Cheat_Sheet.

Python hashlib

Let's take a look at how to use hash functions in Python. Run the following in a Python shell.

```
import hashlib
hashlib.sha512('123456').hexdigest()
```

As output, you should see the hash **ba3253876aed6bc22d4a6ff53 d8406c6ad864195ed144ab5c87621b6c233b548baeae6956df346ec8c17f5ea 10f35ee3cbc514797ed7ddd3145464e2a0bab413**, as shown in the following screenshot:

```
Python 2.7.6 (default, Mar 22 2014, 22:59:56)
[GCC 4.8.2] on linux2
Type "help", "copyright", "credits" or "license" for more in
formation.
>>> import hashlib
>>> hashlib.sha512('123456').hexdigest()
'ba3253876aed6bc22d4a6ff53d8406c6ad864195ed144ab5c87621b6c23
3b548baeae6956df346ec8c17f5ea10f35ee3cbc514797ed7ddd3145464e
2a0bab413'
>>>
```

The random-looking string of hexadecimal characters is the sha512 hash of the '123456' string, and this is what we will store in our database. Every time the user enters the plaintext password, we'll run it through the hash function and verify that the two hashes meet up. If an attacker or employee sees the hash in the database, they cannot masquerade as the user because they cannot deduce '123456' from the hash.

Reversing hashes

Actually, the heading of this section isn't entirely true. While there is no way to *reverse* a hash and write a function that takes the preceding hexadecimal string as input and produces `'123456'` as output, people can be pretty determined. The hacker may still try every possible likely input and run it through the same hash function and keep doing this until the hashes match up. When the hacker comes across an input that produces **ba3253876aed6bc22d4a6ff53d8406c6ad864195ed144ab5c87621b6c233b548 baeae6956df346ec8c17f5ea10f35ee3cbc514797ed7ddd3145464e2a0bab413** as an output, he has effectively cracked the password.

However, hashing functions tend to need a lot of processing power, so it is not practical to run through large amounts of input (known as *brute forcing*). People have also created so-called rainbow tables with all common inputs precomputed and stored in a database so that the results can be found instantly. This is a classic *space-time* trade-off that is so often seen in computer science. If we compute hashes for all possible inputs, it will take a long time; if we want to compute every possible combination in advance so that we can look up the results instantly, we need a lot of storage space.

If you go to a hash reversal website, such as `http://md5decrypt.net/en/Sha512/`, and input the exact hex string you noted here, it'll tell you that the decrypted version is **123456**.

It didn't actually try every possible combination of inputs in the claimed **0.143** seconds, but it stored the answer from a previous time when the hash was computed. Such sites have a large database containing mappings and plaintext strings along with their hashed equivalents.

If you hash a string such as `b^78asdflkjwe@#xx...&AFs[--1` and paste the resulting hash into the md5decrypt website, you'll note that the string is not common enough for this particular site to have precomputed, and instead of getting the plain text back again, you'll get a screen that looks similar to the following screenshot:

We want all of the passwords we store to be complicated enough to not exist in precomputed hash tables. However, our users are more likely to choose passwords that are common enough that they *have* been precomputed. The solution is to add what is known as *salt* to our passwords before we store them.

Salting passwords

As users tend to use weak passwords, such as `123456`, that quite likely exist in precomputed hash tables, we want to do our users a favor and add some random value to their passwords when we store them. This makes it even more difficult for a malicious attacker who has access to the stored hash to gain the user's private password, even though we will store the random value we used with the password. This is known as *salting* the password; similarly to salting food, it is easy for us to add some salt to the password, but removing the salt is hopefully impossible.

In summary, we want to:

- Accept a plaintext password from the user at registration time
- Add some random value (salt) to this password to strengthen it
- Hash the concatenation of the password and salt
- Store the hash and salt

When the user logs in, we need to:

- Take the plaintext password from the user
- Find the stored salt in our database and add it to the user's input
- Hash the concatenation of the password and salt
- Verify that the result matches what we previously stored

Implementing secure password storage in Python

To implement the preceding, we'll create a very small PasswordHelper class that will take care of the hashing and generation of random salts. Although this is very little code, when we use the standard hashlib, os, and base64 Python libraries, it is good practice to abstract all the cryptography logic to its own class. That way, if we change how we implement password management, we can make most of our changes to this new class and not have to touch the main application code.

We also need to make some changes to our login() function, flesh out our registration() function, and create a new method for our database helper code that will add a new user to our mock database.

Creating the PasswordHelper class

Let's start with PasswordHelper. Create a file called passwordhelper.py in your waitercaller directory and add the following code to it:

```python
import hashlib
import os
import base64

class PasswordHelper:

    def get_hash(self, plain):
        return hashlib.sha512(plain).hexdigest()

    def get_salt(self):
        return base64.b64encode(os.urandom(20))

    def validate_password(self, plain, salt, expected):
        return self.get_hash(plain + salt) == expected
```

The first two methods are used when a user registers for the first time and can be explained as follows:

- The `get_hash()` method is just a wrapper of the `sha512` hash function that we looked at earlier. We'll use this to create the final hash that we will store in our database.

- The `get_salt()` method uses `os.urandom()` to generate a cryptographically secure random string. We will encode this as a `base64` string as the random string may contain any bytes, some of which we may have issues with storing in our database.

The `validate_password()` method is used when the user logs in and gives us the original plaintext password again. We'll pass in what the user gave us (the `plain` parameter), the salt that we stored when they registered, and verify that hashing the two produces the same hash that we stored (the `expected` parameter).

Updating our database code

We now need to store a password and salt associated with each user; we can't use the simple e-mail and password dictionary that we had before. Instead, for our mock database, we'll use a list of dictionaries, with every piece of information we need to store having a key and value.

We'll also update the code in `mockdbhelper.py` to read as follows:

```
MOCK_USERS = [{"email": "test@example.com", "salt":
  "8Fb23mMNHD5Zb8pr2qWA3PE9bH0=", "hashed":
  "1736f83698df3f8153c1fbd6ce2840f8aace4f200771a46672635374073cc876c
  "f0aa6a31f780e576578f791b5555b50df46303f0c3a7f2d21f91aa1429ac22e"}]

class MockDBHelper:
    def get_user(self, email):
        user = [x for x in MOCK_USERS if x.get("email") == email]
        if user:
            return user[0]
        return None

    def add_user(self, email, salt, hashed):
MOCK_USERS.append({"email": email, "salt": salt, "hashed":hashed})
```

Our mock user still has the password `123456`, but a potential attacker can no longer work this out by looking up the hash in a rainbow table. We also created the `add_user()` function, which takes the `email`, `salt`, and `hashed` password for a new user and stores a record of this. Our `get_user()` method now needs to loop through all the mock users to find out whether any match the input e-mail address. This is inefficient but will be handled more efficiently by our database, and as we will never have hundreds of mock users, we don't need to worry about this.

Updating our application code

In our main `waitercaller.py` file, we need to add another `import` for our password helper and instantiate a global instance of our password helper class so that we can use it in our `register()` and `login()` functions. We also need to modify our `login()` function to account for the new database model and flesh out our `register()` function to perform some validation and call the database code to add a new user.

Add the following line to the imports section of `waitercaller.py`:

```
from passwordhelper import PasswordHelper
```

Then, add the following near the place where you created the `DBHelper()` object:

```
PH = PasswordHelper()
```

Now, modify the `login()` function to read as follows:

```
@app.route("/login", methods=["POST"])
def login():
    email = request.form.get("email")
    password = request.form.get("password")
    stored_user = DB.get_user(email)
    if stored_user and PH.validate_password(password,
      stored_user['salt'], stored_user['hashed']):

        user = User(email)
        login_user(user, remember=True)
        return redirect(url_for('account'))
    return home()
```

The only real change is in the `if` statement, in which we will now use the password helper to validate the password using the salt and user-provided password. We will also change the variable name of the user to `stored_user` as this is now a dictionary instead of just the password value it used to be.

Finally, we need to build the `register()` function. This will use the password and database helper to create a new salted and hashed password and store this along with the user's e-mail address in our database.

Add a `/register` route and associated function to the `waitercaller.py` file with the following code:

```
@app.route("/register", methods=["POST"])
def register():
    email = request.form.get("email")
    pw1 = request.form.get("password")
    pw2 = request.form.get("password2")
    if not pw1 == pw2:
        return redirect(url_for('home'))
    if DB.get_user(email):
        return redirect(url_for('home'))
    salt = PH.get_salt()
    hashed = PH.get_hash(pw1 + salt)
    DB.add_user(email, salt, hashed)
    return redirect(url_for('home'))
```

We asked the user to input their password twice on our registration form as it's easy for users to make a typo when they register and then not be able to access their account (as they registered with a different password from the one they meant to). Therefore, in this step, we can confirm that the two passwords entered by the user are the same.

We also verified that the user doesn't already exist as each user needs to use a unique e-mail address.

Finally, we generated a salt, created a hash from the password and salt, and stored this in our database. Then, we redirected the user back to homepage, testing our registration functionality.

It's time to give the application a test run again. Close your browser and restart the application locally. Visit the homepage and register an account by choosing an e-mail and password. When you get redirected to the homepage after registration, log in using the same username and password you just registered with. If all went well, you'll see the **You are logged in** message. Again, visit `http://localhost:5000/logout` in order to log out.

Summary

In this chapter, we looked at how to use Bootstrap to make our application look good out of the box and to be responsive based on our user's screen size. We got a basic User Account Control system up and running, and we can register users, log users in, and log them out again.

We also spent some time looking at how to securely store passwords using cryptographic hash functions and salts.

In the next chapter, we'll build out the functionality of our application, which we discussed in the project outline at the start of this chapter. We'll also look at an easier way to create the forms that our visitors will use to interact with our application.

10
Template Inheritance and WTForms in Waiter Caller Project

In the previous chapter, we created a rudimentary user account system. However, we only made a very simple route access controlled — the one that simply showed the string "You are logged in". In this chapter, we'll add some more of the desired functionality, and allow logged-in users to add restaurant tables, see the URLs associated with these tables, and view attention requests from customers. One of the problems we'll come across is that of wanting to reuse the same elements for different pages of our application. You'll see how to solve this problem without code duplication by using Jinja's inheritance system. As mentioned in the previous chapter, we do not communicate very well with our user when mistakes, such as entering an incorrect password, are made. To address this, we'll take a look at another Flask extension, WTForms, and see how it can simplify creating and validating forms.

In this chapter, we'll cover the following topics:

- Adding account and dashboard pages to our application
- Shortening URLs using the bitly API
- Adding functionality for handling attention requests
- Adding user feedback through WTForms

Adding the Account and Dashboard pages

We want to add two new pages to our application: 'Dashboard', where all requests from the patrons of a particular restaurant can be seen, and 'Account', where the restaurants can manage their tables and view the URLs that they need to make available on the tables.

We could simply create two new .html files in our templates directory and write the HTML from scratch. But we'll soon find that we need many of the same elements from our home page (at the very least, the parts that include and configure Bootstrap). Then we'll be tempted to just copy and paste the HTML from the home page and start working on our new page from there.

Introducing Jinja templates

Copying and pasting code is usually a sign that something is wrong. In application code, it means that you haven't modularized your code well, and you need to create some more classes and probably add a couple of import statements to include the reused code wherever it is needed. Using Jinja, we can follow a very similar pattern, by using *template inheritance*. We'll first split our home page into two separate template files, base.html and home.html, with all the elements that we want to reuse in the base file. We can then have all three of our other pages (Home, Account, and Dashboard) inherit from the *base template*, and only write the code that differs across the three.

Jinja handles inheritance by using the concept of *blocks*. Each parent template can have named blocks, and a child that extends a parent can fill in these blocks with its own custom content. The Jinja inheritance system is quite powerful, and accounts for nested blocks and overwriting existing blocks. However, we're only going to scratch the surface of its functionality. We'll have our base template contain all the reusable code, and it'll contain one blank block named content and one named navbar. Each of our three pages will extend from the base template, providing their own version of the content block (for the main page content) and the navigation bar. We'll need to make the navigation bar dynamic, because the **Login** fields of the bar at the top of the page will only appear if the user isn't logged in.

Creating the base template

Create a new file called `base.html` in your `templates` directory, and insert the following code:

```html
<!DOCTYPE html>
<html lang="en">
  <head>
    <meta charset="utf-8">
    <meta http-equiv="X-UA-Compatible" content="IE=edge">
    <meta name="viewport" content="width-device width,
    initial-scale=1">

    <title>Waiter Caller</title>

    <!-- Bootstrap core CSS -->
    <link href="../static/css/bootstrap.min.css" rel="stylesheet">

    <!-- HTML5 shim and Respond.js for IE8 support of HTML5
    elements and media queries -->
    <!--[if lt IE 9]>
      <script src="https://oss.maxcdn.com/html5shiv/3.7.2/
      html5shiv.min.js"></script>
      <script src="https://oss.maxcdn.com/respond/1.4.2/
      respond.min.js"></script>
    <![endif]-->

  </head>
  <body>

    {% block navbar %}
    <nav class="navbar navbar-inverse navbar-fixed-top">
      <div class="container">
        <div class="navbar-header">
          <a class="navbar-brand" href="/dashboard">Dashboard</a>
          <a class="navbar-brand" href="/account">Account</a>
        </div>
      </div>
    </nav>
    {% endblock %}

    {% block content %}
    {% endblock %}
```

```
        <div class="container">

          <hr>
          <footer>
            <p>&copy; A. Non 2015</p>
          </footer>
        </div>
      <!-- Bootstrap core JavaScript

        ================================================== -->
        <!-- Placed at the end of the document so the pages load faster
        -->
        <script    src="https://ajax.googleapis.com/ajax/libs/
          jquery/1.11.3/jquery.min.js"></script>
        <script src="../static/js/bootstrap.min.js"></script>
      </body>
    </html>
```

In the preceding code, we have all our header and our page footer code—elements that will be common across all our pages—in one file. We define two blocks, using the Jinja syntax, which is similar to the other Jinja statements that we have seen, namely:

```
{% block content %}
{% endblock %}
```

And

```
{% block navbar %}
[...]
{% endblock %}
```

In this example, `content` and `navbar` are the names of our blocks, and we can choose these freely, while `block` and `endblock` are Jinja keywords, and the `{% %}` symbols are used to indicate the Jinja statements as in earlier examples. This is in itself a completely valid Jinja template; even though the content block is empty, we can render the template directly from our Flask app, and we would see a page that simply pretended that the content block didn't exist.

We can also extend this template, though; that is, we can create children using it as the parent. Children have the option of *overwriting* any of the specified blocks simply by declaring them again. We declared `navbar` as a block as our home page will use the navigation bar that we wrote earlier—the one that includes a login form. Once logged in, however, our pages for dashboard and account will have exactly the same navigation bar—the one we define in our base template.

Creating the dashboard template

Our dashboard page will eventually show all customers' requests for service so that a waiter can easily see which tables need attention. For now though, we'll just create an outline of the page. Create a new file in your `templates` directory called `dashboard.html`, and add the following code:

```
{% extends "base.html" %}

{% block content %}
    <div class="jumbotron">
      <div class="container">
        <h1>Dashboard</h1>
        <p>View all patron requests below</p>
      </div>
    </div>

    <div class="container">
      <div class="row">
        <div class="col-md-12">
          <h2>Requests</h2>
          <p>All your customers are currently satisfied - no
          requests</p>
        </div>
      </div>
    </div>
{% endblock %}
```

The most important line in the preceding code snippet is the first one—we use the Jinja `extends` keyword to indicate that this template should inherit all the code contained in another template. The keyword is followed by the filename of the template to inherit from, contained within inverted commas.

Following that, we simply create the content block in exactly the same way we did in our base template. This time, instead of leaving it blank, we add some HTML to be displayed on our dashboard page.

Creating the account template

The account page will be the one where the user can add new tables, delete tables, or get the URL for the existing tables. Again, as we do not yet have any application code to represent a table, we'll just create an outline of the page. Create a file called `account.html` in your `templates` directory, and add the following code:

```
{% extends "base.html" %}

{% block content %}
    <div class="jumbotron">
```

```
      <div class="container">
        <h1>Account</h1>
        <p>Manage tables and get URLs</p>
      </div>
    </div>

    <div class="container">
      <div class="row">
        <div class="col-md-12">
          <h2>Tables</h2>

        </div>
      </div>
    </div>
  {% endblock %}
```

Creating the home template

The home.html template contains the entire code specific to our home page, and which isn't part of the base template. The code can be seen in the code bundle as templates/home_1.html, but is not included here as it is too long. Have a look at it and see how we define a new navbar block which contains the login form, and which overrides the default one provided in the base template. Similarly, it defines the content block, which replaces the empty content block that we defined in our base template. The end result hasn't changed—we'll still see exactly the same home page, but now the code is split between the base.html and home.html files, allowing us to reuse large parts of it for the new pages that we created previously.

Adding the routing code

We need our Python code to return the new template files when /account and /dashboard are visited. Add the dashboard() function to your waitercaller.py file, and modify the account function() to read as follows:

```
@app.route("/dashboard")
@login_required
def dashboard():
  return render_template("dashboard.html")

@app.route("/account")
@login_required
def account():
  return render_template("account.html")
```

Give the new pages a go! Start the application locally as before, by running:

```
python waitercaller.py
```

Navigate to `http://localhost:5000` to see the home page. Log in using the form, and now, instead of the bare message we had before, you should see a nicer looking skeleton of the **Account** page, as seen in the following image:

Click on the **Dashboard** link in the navigation bar at the top, and you should see the skeleton for that page, too, as seen in the following image:

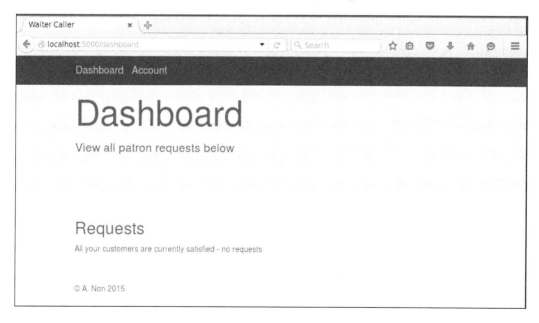

Creating restaurant tables

Now we need to introduce the concept of a *table* to our application, and be able to represent this both in our database and in our application code. A table should have the following attributes:

- An ID number that uniquely identifies that table across all users of our app
- A name that is user-definable and unique within a specific user's tables
- An owner so that we will know to which user a table belongs

If we were following an **Object Oriented Programming** style religiously, we would create a `Table` class which had these properties. We would then also create a bunch of other classes for everything in our application. Following this approach, we would also create methods to serialize each of our objects into something that can be stored in our database, and more methods to *deserialize* them from the database back to objects.

For the sake of brevity, and because our model is simple enough, we'll be taking a shortcut that is sure to offend some, and simply use Python dictionaries to represent most of our objects. We'll see when we add MongoDB to our application that these dictionaries will be trivial to write to and read from the database.

Writing the restaurant table code

Let's have a brief look at what our tables need to do. First, the user of our app will need to be able to add and remove new tables on the `account` page—both initially when an account is registered and later if changes need to be made. Secondly, the user should be able to view the URL associated with each table, so that these URLs can be printed and made available at the physical tables. When a new table is added, we'll need to create a mock database.

We'll start by providing our users with an input box on the `account` page, where they can input the name or number of a new table in order to create it. When a new table is created, we'll create a unique ID number and use that to create a new URL. We'll then use the bitly API to create a shortened version of the URL—one that our users' patrons will be able to type into a smartphone more easily. We'll then store the table name, ID, and shortened URL in our mock database.

Adding the create table form

In the `account.html` template, add the following directly beneath the line `<h2>Tables</h2>`:

```
<h2>Add new table</h2>
<form class="form-inline" action="/account/createtable"
method="POST">
```

```
        <input type="text" name="tablenumber"
        placeholder="Table number or name" class="form-control">
        <input type="submit" value="Create" class="btn btn-primary">
    </form>
```

This is a very basic form with a single input for a new table name and a button
to submit the form. If you load the application and navigate to the **Account** page,
you should now see something like the following image:

Adding the create table route

Creating a table backend is not too complicated, but it has subtleties that are important
to understand. First, our users can give the table any name they want. For most users,
these names will probably just be incrementing numbers starting from 1 and ending
at the number of tables in the restaurant, as this is a common way for restaurants to
name their tables. Because many restaurant managers will be using our application,
we can't assume that these names will be unique across all accounts. Most users of our
application will probably have a table called 1. Therefore, when a restaurant patron
indicates that he or she is at Table 1 and wants service, we have to be able to pick the
correct Table 1 from potentially many restaurants. To solve this, each table in our
database will have a unique ID that we'll use for table identification in the URLs, but
we'll display the user-chosen name (for example, 1) on the **Account** page to allow our
users to easily manage their personal list of tables.

When we insert a new item into our database, we'll get the unique ID of that
item. But, because we want to use the ID as part of the URL, we get into a sort of
chicken-or-egg-first situation where we need to insert the table into the database in
order to get the ID, but we also need the ID in order to create the URL before we can
properly insert the table into the database.

To solve this problem, we have to insert a half-created table into our database to get
the ID, then use the ID to create the URL, and then update the table we just created
to associate it with the URL.

Add the following route to your `waitercaller.py` file which does this (or rather, will do this once we've created the required functions in our database code):

```
@app.route("/account/createtable", methods=["POST"])
@login_required
def account_createtable():
    tablename = request.form.get("tablenumber")
    tableid = DB.add_table(tablename, current_user.get_id())
    new_url = config.base_url + "newrequest/" + tableid
    DB.update_table(tableid, new_url)
    return redirect(url_for('account'))
```

Note that we structure all the functionality of our application that is related to our account page under a `sub-route` `/account/`. We preface the function name for routes that belong to the account with `account_`. This helps us have clearer sections in our application code, which can become messy and unmaintainable as we add more and more routes.

We have to associate each table with an owner, so we use the `FlaskLogin current_user` functionality to get the currently logged-in user's ID. We're also going to use our `config.py` file to define the base URL to be associated with the tables.

Add the following imports to `waitercaller.py` in order to use the `current_user` functionality and access our `config`:

```
from flask.ext.login import current_user
import config
```

Add the following to the `config.py` file (remember, this isn't part of the Git repository, so this value is only used for local development):

```
base_url = "http://127.0.0.1:5000/"
```

The preceding URL is exactly equivalent to `localhost:5000` that we've been using, as `127.0.0.1` is a special IP address that always points back to your own machine. However, we'll use an IP address in our `config` instead of `localhost` to maintain compatibility with the Bitly API that we'll use in the next section, *Shortening URL's using the bitly API*, of this chapter.

Adding the create table database code

The mock database code for our tables is similar to that for our users and passwords. Create the following list of dictionaries at the top of the `mockdbhelper.py` file to store your tables:

```
MOCK_TABLES = [{"_id": "1", "number": "1", "owner":
"test@example.com","url": "mockurl"}]
```

The preceding code also creates a single table, 1, and assigns it to our mock user. Note that 1, which is the value of the _id key, is the ID number that, for our production system, will be unique across all user accounts. The 1 that is the value of the number key is the user-chosen value that might be duplicated across different users of our system. Because we only have one test user, we'll simplify our mock code, and always use the same value for both the unique ID and the user-chosen number.

For our mock database, adding a table is simply appending a new dictionary that represents a table to our list of existing mock tables. Add the following method to the mockdbhelper.py file:

```
def add_table(self, number, owner):
    MOCK_TABLES.append({"_id": number, "number": number, "owner":
    owner})
    return number
```

We return number from this function, which is the mock ID. In our test code, this is the same value that was input to this function. In our real code, this number will be the generated ID, and will be different from the input.

Finally, we need to add the update_table() method that will allow us to associate a URL with a table. Add the following method to mockdbhelper.py:

```
def update_table(self, _id, url):
    for table in MOCK_TABLES:
        if table.get("_id") == _id:
            table["url"] = url
            break
```

Our application code gives the preceding method both the table ID generated by the add_table() method and the URL to associate with the table. The update_table() method then finds the correct table and associates the URL with the table. Again, the for loop through a list might look inefficient as opposed to using a dictionary, but it's important for our mock database code to use the same ideas as the real database code that we'll write in the next chapter. As our real database will store a collection of tables, our mock code emulates this by storing them in a list.

Adding the view table database code

We now have the functionality for adding new tables in place, but we can't see them yet. We want all the existing tables to be listed on the account page so that we can see which tables exist, have the ability to delete them, and view their URLs.

Adding the following method to `mockdbhelper.py` will allow us to access the existing tables of a specific user:

```
def get_tables(self, owner_id):
    return MOCK_TABLES
```

Again, we simplify and have our test code ignore the `owner_id` argument and return all the tables (as we only have one test user). However, it's important that our mock methods take the same inputs and outputs as our real methods will, as we don't want our application code to be aware of whether it is running production or test code.

Modifying the account route to pass table data

We should get the latest information about the tables from the database and display these tables to the user each time our account page is loaded. Modify the `/account` route in `waitercaller.py` to look as follows:

```
@app.route("/account")
@login_required
def account():
    tables = DB.get_tables(current_user.get_id())
    return render_template("account.html", tables=tables)
```

This preceding method now gets the tables from the database and passes the data through to the template.

Modifying the template to show the tables

Our template now has access to the table data, so all we need to do is to loop through each table and display the relevant information. The terminology used could get a bit confusing at this point, as we will use an HTML table to display information about our virtual restaurant tables, even though the uses of the word table are unrelated. HTML tables are a way to display tabulated data, which in our case is data about the restaurant tables.

In the `account.html` file, add the following code beneath the line `<h2>tables</h2>`:

```
<table class="table table-striped">
  <tr>
    <th>No.</th>
    <th>URL</th>
    <th>Delete</th>
  </tr>
  {% for table in tables %}
    <form class="form-inline" action="/account/deletetable">
```

```
<tr>
  <td>{{table.number}}</td>
  <td>{{table.url}}</td>
  <td><input type="submit" value="Delete"
  class="form-control"></td>
  <input type="text" name="tableid"
  value="{{table._id}}" hidden>
</tr>
</form>
{% endfor %}
</table>
```

The preceding code creates a simple table of tables, displaying the table number (user chosen), the URL, and a delete button for each table. Each table is, in fact, a form that submits a request to delete that specific table. In order to do this, we also use a hidden input containing the unique ID of each table. This ID is passed along with the delete request so that our application code knows which table to delete from the database.

Adding the delete table route to our backend code

Add the following route to your `waitercaller.py` file, which simply accepts the table ID that needs to be deleted and then asks the database to delete it:

```
@app.route("/account/deletetable")
@login_required
def account_deletetable():
  tableid = request.args.get("tableid")
  DB.delete_table(tableid)
  return redirect(url_for('account'))
```

Create the following method in `mockdbhelper.py`, which accepts a table ID and deletes that table:

```
def delete_table(self, table_id):
    for i, table in enumerate(MOCK_TABLES):
        if table.get("_id") == table_id:
            del MOCK_TABLES[i]
          break
```

Similar to the update code that we wrote earlier, it's necessary to loop through the mock tables to find the one with the correct ID before we can delete it.

Testing the restaurant table code

We've added quite a lot of code to our application. Since a lot of the different sections of code that we've added depend on each other, it has been difficult to actually run the code while writing it. However, now we have the functionality to create, view, and delete tables, so we can now give our application another test run. Fire up the application, log in, and navigate to the **Account** page. You should see the single mock table and be able to add more using the create table form. Play around by adding new tables and deleting the existing ones. When you add tables, they should get a URL associated with them based on their number (remember that for our production application, this number will be a long unique identifier instead of simply the number that we choose for our table). The interface should look like the following image:

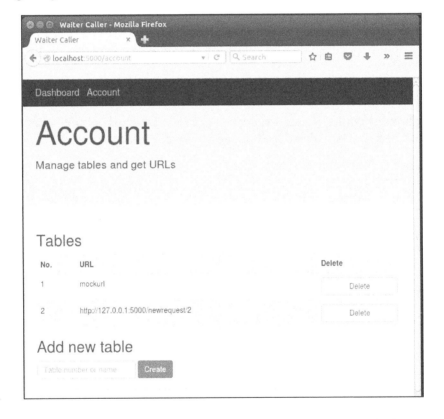

Also take another look at the mobile view for this page by resizing the browser window, making it narrow enough to trigger the layout switch. Note that because we've used Bootstrap's responsive layout features, the **Delete** buttons shunt up closer to the URLs and the **Create** button moves beneath the text input, as in the following image:

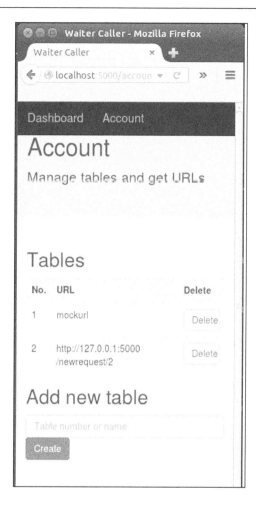

This might not look quite as good as the full-sized view, but it'll certainly be helpful to our visitors who want to use our site from their phones, as they won't need to worry about zooming in or scrolling sideways to access all the functionality of our site.

Shortening URLs using the bitly API

Our users will not want to type in the long URLs that we currently provide for calling a waiter to their table. We'll now look at using the bitly API to create shorter equivalents of the URLs that we've already created. The shorter URLs, which can be typed into address bars (especially on mobile devices) more easily, will then be shown as being associated with the corresponding tables instead of the longer ones we have now.

Introducing Bitly

The premise behind Bitly—and many similar services—is simple. Given a URL of arbitrary length, the service returns a shorter URL of the form `bit.ly/XySDj72`. Bitly and similar services normally have very short root domains (`bit.ly` is five letters), and they simply maintain a database that links the short URLs they create to the longer ones input by the users. Because they use a combination of lower- and uppercase characters as well as digits to create the shortened URLs, there is no shortage of combinations to use, even while keeping the total length of the URL very short.

Using the bitly API

As with the other APIs that we have used, bitly is free to use within certain limitations, but requires registration in order to get an API token. The bitly API is accessed over HTTPS and returns JSON responses (similar to what we've seen before). To interface with the API, we'll use a few lines of Python along with the `urllib2` and `json` standard libraries.

Getting a bitly oauth token

At the time of writing, bitly offers two ways of authenticating with their API. The first is to use an API token given to you when you register. The second way is to use an oauth token. As API tokens are being deprecated by bitly, we'll be using an oauth token.

The first step is to register an account on `bitly.com` and confirm your e-mail address. Simply head over to `bitly.com`, hit the **Sign up** button, and give a username, e-mail address and password. Click the confirmation link that they send to the provided e-mail, and sign in to your bitly account.

To register for an oauth token, go to `https://bitly.com/a/oauth_apps` and enter your password again when prompted. You should now see your new oauth token displayed on the screen. Copy this, as we'll need it in the Python code that we're about to write. It should look something like this:

```
ad922578a7a1c6065a3bb91bd62b02e52199afdb
```

Creating the bitlyhelper file

Following the pattern we've used throughout the building of this web application, we'll create a `BitlyHelper` class to shorten the URLs. Again, this is good practice, as it allows us to easily replace just this module with another link shortening service if we ever need to. Create a file named `bitlyhelper.py` in your `waitercaller` directory and add the following code, substituting your bitly oauth token as appropriate. The token in the following snippet is valid for this Waiter Caller application. You should substitute the token that you received by following the steps outlined above.

```
import urllib2
import json

TOKEN = "cc922578a7a1c6065a2aa91bc62b02e41a99afdb"
ROOT_URL = "https://api-ssl.bitly.com"
SHORTEN = "/v3/shorten?access_token={}&longUrl={}"


class BitlyHelper:

    def shorten_url(self, longurl):
        try:
            url = ROOT_URL + SHORTEN.format(TOKEN, longurl)
            response = urllib2.urlopen(url).read()
            jr = json.loads(response)
            return jr['data']['url']
        except Exception as e:
            print e
```

This class, `BitlyHelper`, provides a single method that takes in a long URL and returns a short one. There should be nothing about the last code snippet that is difficult to understand, as it only uses the ideas we've already seen while using JSON-based APIs over HTTP.

Using the bitly module

To use our bitly code, we simply need to create a `BitlyHelper` object in our main application code, and then use it to create a short URL every time a new restaurant table is created. Modify the globals section of `waitercaller.py` as follows:

```
DB = DBHelper()
PH = PasswordHelper()
BH = BitlyHelper()
```

And add the import for `BitlyHelper()` to the imports section of `waitercaller.py`:

```
from bitlyhelper import BitlyHelper
```

Now modify the `createtable` method to read as follows:

```
@app.route("/account/createtable", methods=["POST"])
@login_required
def account_createtable():
    tablename = request.form.get("tablenumber")
    tableid = DB.add_table(tablename, current_user.get_id())
    new_url = BH.shorten_url(config.base_url + "newrequest/" +
    tableid)

    DB.update_table(tableid, new_url)
    return redirect(url_for('account'))
```

Fire up the app and go to the account page again. Create a new table, and you should see that the URL of the new table is a bitly URL. If you visit this URL in the browser, you'll see that it automatically redirects to something like `http://127.0.0.1/newrequest/2` (which, in turn, should throw a server error at this point).

Now that we can associate a short URL with every new table created, we need to add the idea of a *request* to our application, so that when our users' patrons visit these URLs, we notify the restaurant of the request for attention.

Adding functionality to handle attention requests

We need to deal with two aspects of attention requests. The first, as discussed earlier, is to create new requests when a user visits a URL. The second is to allow the waiters of the restaurant to view these requests and mark them as resolved.

Writing the attention request code

When a user visits a URL, we should create an attention request and store it in the database. This attention request should contain:

- The time the request was made
- The table from which the request was made

As before, we'll just use a Python dictionary to represent the *attention request object*. We need to have our application code create new attention requests and allow these requests to be added, retrieved, and deleted from the database.

Adding the attention request route

Add the following route to `waitercaller.py`:

```
@app.route("/newrequest/<tid>")
def new_request(tid):
  DB.add_request(tid, datetime.datetime.now())
  return "Your request has been logged and a waiter will be with
  you shortly"
```

This route matches a dynamic table ID. Since our URLs use the globally unique table ID and not the user-chosen table number, we don't need to worry about which restaurant owns the table. We tell our database to create a new request, which contains the table ID and the current time. We then display a message to the patron, notifying him or her that the request was successfully made. Note that this is the only route for the application that our users' patrons will use. The rest of the routes are all intended to be used only by the restaurant managers or waiters themselves.

We also need the Python `datetime` module to get the current time. Add the following line to your imports section in `waitercaller.py`:

```
import datetime
```

Adding the attention request database code

The database code for the attention requests uses the same ideas as the code we recently added for dealing with restaurant tables. Add the following global at the top of `mockdbhelper.py`:

```
MOCK_REQUESTS = [{"_id": "1", "table_number": "1","table_id": "1",
  "time": datetime.datetime.now()}]
```

The preceding global creates a single mock attention request for table number 1 (an existing mock table) and sets the time of the request to be the time when we started the `waitercaller` app by running:

python waitercaller.py

Whenever we make changes to our app during development, the server restarts, and this time will also be updated to the current time whenever this happens.

We also need to add the import for the `datetime` module to the top of the `dbconfig.py` file:

```
import datetime
```

For the actual `add_request()` method, it is again important to distinguish between the table number (user chosen) and the table ID (globally unique across all our users). The URL used for creating the request made use of the globally unique ID, but the waiters will want to see the human readable table name next to the request notification. At the time of adding a request, we therefore find the table number associated with the table ID and include that as part of the stored request.

Add the following method to `mockdbhelper.py`:

```
def add_table(self, number, owner):
    MOCK_TABLES.append(
        {"_id": str(number), "number": number, "owner":
        owner})
    return number
```

Again, we use `table_id` as the unique ID for our dictionary that represents a request. As before, when we add a real database, we will generate a new request ID here, which will not be the same as our table ID.

Add the get and delete methods for attention requests

While we are editing the database code, add the following methods as well:

```
def get_requests(self, owner_id):
    return MOCK_REQUESTS

def delete_request(self, request_id):
    for i, request [...]
        if requests [...]
            del MOCK_REQUESTS[i]
            break
```

The first method gets all attention requests for a specific user and will be used to populate our dashboard page with all the unresolved requests that require attention from waiters. The second deletes a specific request and will be used (also from the dashboard page) when waiters mark a request as resolved.

 If our Waiter Caller application aimed to provide more advanced functionality, we might add a property to requests to mark them as resolved, instead of deleting them outright. If we wanted to provide an analysis on how many requests were being made, how long they took on an average to be resolved, and so on, then keeping the resolved requests would be essential. For our simple implementation, resolved requests are of no further use, and we simply delete them.

Modifying the dashboard route to use attention requests

When the restaurant manager or waiter opens the dashboard of the app, they should see all current attention requests along with the time when the request was made (so that the patrons who have been waiting for longer can be prioritized). We have the time the request was logged, so we'll calculate the time elapsed since the request was made.

Modify the `dashboard()` route in `waitercaller.py` to read as follows:

```
@app.route("/dashboard")
@login_required
def dashboard():
    now = datetime.datetime.now()
    requests = DB.get_requests(current_user.get_id())
    for req in requests:
        deltaseconds = (now - req['time']).seconds
        req['wait_minutes'] = "{}.{}".format((deltaseconds/60),
            str(deltaseconds % 60).zfill(2))
    return render_template("dashboard.html", requests=requests)
```

The modified `dashboard()` route grabs all the attention requests that belong to the currently logged in user, using `current_user.get_id()` as before. We calculate a *delta time* for each request (the current time minus the request time) and add this as an attribute for each request in our requests list. Then we pass the updated list through to the template.

Modifying the template code to display attention requests

We want our dashboard code to check if any attention requests exist and then to display each of these in a way similar to the way the tables are displayed on the account page. Every attention request should have a **Resolve** button to allow the waiter to indicate that he has dealt with the request.

If no attention requests exist, we should display the same message we had displayed on the dashboard page previously, indicating that all the patrons are currently satisfied.

Add the following code to the body of `dashboard.html`, removing the placeholder statement that we added previously:

```
<h2>Requests</h2>
{% if requests %}
  <table class="table table-striped">
    <tr>
      <th>No.</th>
      <th>Wait</th>
      <th>Resolve</th>
    </tr>
    {% for request in requests %}
      <tr>
        <form class="form-inline" action="/dashboard/resolve">
          <td>{{request.table_number}}</td>
          <td>{{request.wait_minutes}}</td>
          <input type="text" name="request_id"
          value="{{request._id}}" hidden>
          <td><input type="submit" value="Resolve"
          class="btn btn-primary"></td>
        </form>
      </tr>
    {% endfor %}
  </table>
{% else %}
  <p>All your customers are currently satisfied - no requests</p>
{% endif %}
```

The preceding code is very similar to the table code we saw for the `accounts` template. Instead of the **Delete** button, we have a **Resolve** button, which similarly uses a hidden text input containing the request ID to resolve the correct attention request.

Adding the resolve request application code

Let's add the application code to handle resolving requests. Similar to the way we used the sub-route `/account` for all our account functionality, we use `/dashboard` in the form discussed earlier. Add the following route to `waitercaller.py`:

```
@app.route("/dashboard/resolve")
@login_required
def dashboard_resolve():
    request_id = request.args.get("request_id")
    DB.delete_request(request_id)
    return redirect(url_for('dashboard'))
```

We've already added the database code to remove an attention request, so here we simply need to call that code with the correct request ID, which we have from the hidden field in our template.

With that, most of the functionality of our application should be testable. Let's try it out!

Testing the attention request code

Fire up the app, and test out all the new functionality. First, navigate to the **Account** page and then, in a new tab, navigate to the URL listed for the test table (or add a new table and use the new URL to retest the earlier code as well). You should see the '**Your request has been logged and a waiter will be with you shortly**' message as in the following image:

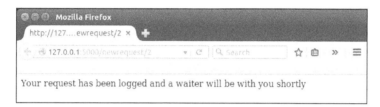

Now go back to the application and navigate to the **Dashboard** page. You should see the mock request as well as the new request you just created by visiting the URL, as seen in the following screenshot:

Refresh the page and note that the values in the '**Wait**' column get incremented appropriately (every refresh will recalculate the deltas in the application code).

Auto-refreshing the dashboard page

The waiters will not want to constantly refresh the dashboard in order to check for new requests and to update the wait times on the existing one. We'll add a meta HTML tag to tell the browser that the page should be refreshed at regular intervals. We'll add a generic placeholder for meta tags in our base template and then override it with the refresh tag in our `dashboard.html` template.

In the `dashboard.html` file, add a Jinja block that contains the meta HTML tag above the content block:

```
{% extends "base.html" %}
{% block metarefresh %} <meta http-equiv="refresh" content="10" > {%
endblock %}

{% block content %}
```

Meta HTML tags indicate messages that don't directly relate to the content that we are serving. They can also be used to add information about the author of a page or to give a list of keywords that search engines may use while indexing the page. In our case, we're specifying a meta tag that asks the browser to refresh every ten seconds.

In the `base.html` file, create an equivalent empty placeholder:

```
{% block metarefresh %} {% endblock %}

<title>Waiter Caller</title>
```

Now open the app in your browser again and navigate to the dashboard page. Every 10 seconds, you should see the page refresh and the wait times update. If you create new attention requests, you'll see these appear after the automatic refresh as well.

Adding user feedback with WTForms

We now have a web application that is largely functional, but still fails to provide the user with helpful feedback, especially when it comes to submitting web forms. Let's look at how to make our application more intuitive by providing feedback when the user succeeds or fails to complete various actions.

To make our life easier, we'll use another Flask add-on, WTForms, which lets us validate inputs by using prespecified patterns or by creating our own. We'll use WTForms to implement all our web forms, namely:

- The registration form
- The sign-in form
- The create table form

Introducing WTForms

You might have noticed that creating the registration form for new users to sign up for our web app was a bit cumbersome. We had to create the HTML form in our template file and then fetch all the input data when the form was submitted in our Python backend code. In order to do this, we had to use the same strings, such as `email` and `password`, in our HTML code (for the `name` attribute) and in our Python code (to load the data from the various fields into variables). These strings, `email` and `password`, are examples of what are sometimes called *magic strings*. It might seem obvious to us, while creating the application, that the strings have to be the same in both the files, but to another developer who might need to maintain the application in the future, or even to our future selves, this implicit link might be a lot less obvious and more confusing.

Furthermore, we had to use a fairly ugly `if` statement in our application code to make sure that the passwords matched. It turns out that we want to do much more validation on user input than just checking that the passwords match. We probably want to also validate that the e-mail address looks like an e-mail address, that the password isn't too short, and possibly more besides. As our user-input forms get longer, and the validation rules get more complicated, we can see that our application code would quickly get pretty messy if we carried on developing forms as we have been doing so far.

Finally, as mentioned earlier, our forms failed to provide the user with helpful feedback when things went wrong.

WTForms solves all of these problems in a simple and intuitive way. We'll soon explain how to create Python classes to represent forms. These classes will contain validation rules, field types, field names, and feedback messages, all in the same place. Our Jinja templates and our application code can then use the *same object* to render the form (when the user views the page) and to process the input (when the user submits the form). Using WTForms therefore allows us to keep our code cleaner and to speed up development. We'll take a quick look at installing WTForms for Flask, before diving into how we can use it for improving our application.

Note that WTForms is a general Python web development add-on that works with many different Python web development frameworks (such as Flask, Django, and others) and template managers (such as Jinja2, Mako, and others). We'll install a Flask-specific extension that will install WTForms and make it easy to interface with our Flask application.

Installing Flask-WTF

We need to install the WTForms add-on for Flask. This is done in the same way as our previous extensions. Simply run the following command (as always, remembering to do it both locally and on your VPS):

```
pip install --user Flask-WTF
```

Creating the registration form

Now let's take a look at building forms. We'll be building a few forms, so we'll create a new Python file in our project to hold all of these. In your `waitercaller` directory, create a file called `forms.py` and add the following code:

```python
from flask_wtf import Form
from wtforms import PasswordField
from wtforms import SubmitField
from wtforms.fields.html5 import EmailField
from wtforms import validators

class RegistrationForm(Form):
    email = EmailField('email',
    validators=[validators.DataRequired(), validators.Email()])
    password = PasswordField('password',
    validators=[validators.DataRequired(),
    validators.Length(min=8, message="Please choose a password
    of at least 8 characters")])
    password2 = PasswordField('password2',
    validators=[validators.DataRequired(),
    validators.EqualTo('password', message='Passwords must
    match')])
    submit = SubmitField('submit', [validators.DataRequired()])
```

The class, `RegistrationForm`, inherits from `Form`, a generic form object that we find inside the `flask_wtf` extension. Everything else is from the `wtforms` module directly (and not from the Flask-specific extension). The form is built from a number of different fields—in our case, an `EmailField`, two `PasswordFields`, and a `Submit` field. All of these will be rendered as their HTML equivalents in our template. We assign each of these desired fields to variables.

We'll use these variables to render the fields and to retrieve data from the fields. Each time we create a field, we pass in some arguments. The first is a string argument to name the form. The second argument is a list of Validators. **Validators** are sets of rules that we can use to differentiate between valid input and invalid input. WTForms provides all the validators that we need, but it's also easy to write custom validators. We use the following validators:

- `DataRequired`: This simply means that if the field is left blank, the form is invalid for all fields.

- `Email`: This uses a regular expression to ensure that the e-mail address is made up of alphanumeric characters, and has an @ symbol and a full-stop in their appropriate places. (Fun fact: this is a surprisingly complicated problem! See `http://www.regular-expressions.info/email.html`.)

- `EqualTo`: This ensures that the data entered in the field is the same as the data entered into another field.

- `Length`: This validator takes optional min and max arguments to define the number of characters the data should contain. We set this to a minimum of 8 to ensure that our users don't pick very weak passwords.

Recall our discussion of the trade-offs between backend and frontend validation and note that these are all backend validation methods, completed server-side. Therefore, it is still worthwhile to add the `Email` validator even if the user's browser supports HTML5; the fact that it is an `email` field will prevent the user from submitting an invalid e-mail address (using a frontend validation check).

Another thing about validators is that we can add a message argument for each validator—not just for each field—and each field can have more than one validator. We'll see later how to display this message to the user if that specific validation check fails.

It's important to note that the variable names you choose for each form field (`email`, `password`, and `password2` in the registration form that we created previously) are more important than most variable names because the `name` and `id` attributes for the final HTML field will be taken from the variable names.

Rendering the registration form

The next step is to use our form object for rendering an empty registration form when a user loads our home page. To do this, we have to modify both our application code (to create an instance of the registration form class and pass it to the template) and our frontend code (to render our fields from the variables of the class, instead of hardcoding them in HTML).

Updating the application code

In our `waitercaller.py` file, we need to import the form we created, instantiate it, and pass it to our template.

Add an import for our registration form:

```
from forms import RegistrationForm
```

Now instantiate the form in our `home()` function and pass the form on to the template. The final `home()` function should read as follows:

```
@app.route("/")
def home():
  registrationform = RegistrationForm()
  return render_template("home.html",
  registrationform=registrationform)
```

Updating the template code

Now that our template has access to an instantiated `RegistrationForm` object, we can use Jinja to render the fields of our form. Update the registration form in `home.html` to read as follows:

```
<h2>Register now</h2>
<form class="form-horizontal" action="/register" method="POST">
  {{ registrationform.csrf_token }}
    <div class="form-group">
      <div class="col-sm-9">
        {{ registrationform.email(class="form-control",
        placeholder="Email Address" )}}
      </div>
    </div>
    <div class="form-group">
      <div class="col-sm-9">
        {{ registrationform.password(class="form-control",
        placeholder="Password" )}}
      </div>
    </div>
    <div class="form-group">
      <div class="col-sm-9">
        {{ registrationform.password2(class="form-control",
        placeholder="Confirm Password" )}}
      </div>
    </div>
    <div class="form-group">
```

```
      <div class="col-sm-9">
        {{ registrationform.submit(class="btn btn-primary
        btn-block")}}
      </div>
    </div>
  </form>
```

The Bootstrap boilerplate (the div tags specifying Bootstrap classes) remains unchanged, but now, instead of creating input fields in HTML, we call functions belonging to our `registrationform` variable that was passed in from the `home()` route. Each variable that we declared in our `RegistrationForm` class (email, password, password2, and submit) is available as a function to which we can pass additional HTML attributes as arguments. The name and id attributes will be set automatically based on the variable names we provided when we wrote the form, and we can add further attributes, such as `class` and `placeholder` by passing them in here. As before, we use 'form-control' as the class of our inputs, and also specify the 'placeholder' values to prompt the user to input information.

We also render the `csrf_token` field at the beginning of the new code. This is a very useful security default that WTForms provides. One of the more common web application vulnerabilities is called **Cross Site Request Forgery** (CSRF). Although a detailed description of this vulnerability falls outside the scope of this book, in short, it exploits the fact that cookies are implemented at the browser level rather than at a web page level. Because cookies are used for authentication, if you log into your one site that is vulnerable to CSRF, and then in a new tab, navigate to a malicious site that can exploit a CSRF vulnerability, the malicious site can carry out actions on the vulnerable site on your behalf. This is achieved by sending across the legitimate cookie (that you created when you logged into the vulnerable site), along with an action that requires authentication. In the worst case scenario, the vulnerable site is your online banking, and the malicious site carries out financial transactions on your behalf, without your knowledge, using the CSRF vulnerability. The CSRF token mitigates against this vulnerability by adding a hidden field to every form with a cryptographically secure set of randomly generated characters. Because the malicious site cannot access this hidden field (even though it can access our cookies), we know that a POST request that includes these characters originates from our site, and not a malicious third-party one. If you find this level of web application security interesting, read more about the CSRF vulnerability on the **Open Web Application Security Project (OWASP)** website (https://www.owasp.org/index.php/Cross-Site_Request_Forgery_(CSRF)). Either way, you should always include the CSRF field in all forms — in fact, the validation step will fail if you omit it.

Testing the new form

Because we used the same Id and name attributes for our form as we did before, our application code for handling the processing of data when the form is submitted will still work. Therefore, fire up the application and make sure that everything is still working at this point. If all has gone well, the home page of the application will look identical to when we last tested our application. You should also be able to use your browser's 'view source' function to check that the various form fields were converted into various HTML input types as expected.

Using WTForms in our application code

The next step is to update our application code to use WTForms for catching data that has been input through the form. Now, instead of having to remember which "name" attributes we used, we can simply instantiate a new `RegistrationForm` object and populate it from the post data received backend. We can also easily run all our validation rules and get a list of errors for each field.

In `waitercaller.py`, modify the `register()` function to read as follows:

```
@app.route("/register", methods=["POST"])
def register():
  form = RegistrationForm(request.form)
  if form.validate():
    if DB.get_user(form.email.data):
      form.email.errors.append("Email address already registered")
      return render_template('home.html', registrationform=form)
    salt = PH.get_salt()
    hashed = PH.get_hash(form.password2.data + salt)
    DB.add_user(form.email.data, salt, hashed)
    return redirect(url_for("home"))
  return render_template("home.html", registrationform=form)
```

In the preceding code, the first change is the first line of the function. We instantiate a new `RegistrationForm` and populate it by passing in the `request.form` object, from which we previously pulled each field individually. As mentioned before, it's great that we don't have to hardcode the field names now! We can instead access the user's input data through the forms properties, such as `form.email.data`.

The second line is also a big change. We can call `form.validate()` to run all our validation rules, and this will return `True` only if all the rules pass, else it will populate the form object with all the relevant failure messages. The last line of the function, therefore, will only get called if there are validation errors. In this case, we now re-render our home page template, passing across a fresh copy of the form (which now has a reference to the errors. We'll see how to display these in the next step).

If the e-mail address is found in our database, we now append an error message to the error messages for the e-mail field and re-render the template to pass this error back to the frontend.

Note that previously, our three return options were all simply redirected to the home page, made using the Flask `redirect()` function. Now we have replaced them all with `render_template()` calls, as we need to pass the new form (with the error messages added) along to the frontend.

Displaying errors to our user

The final step for our new registration form is to display any errors to the user so that the user can fix them and resubmit the form. To do this, we'll add some Jinja `if` statements to our template to check if any errors exist in the form object and display them if they do. Then we'll add some CSS to make these errors appear in red. Finally, we'll look at how we could do all of this more concisely (which we'd definitely want if we had more and larger forms).

Displaying the errors in our template

All we need to do to display the errors is add an `if` statement above each of our input fields, checking if there are any errors to display for that field (remember WTForms automatically populates the error lists for our form object when we run the `validate()` method). If we find errors to display for that field, we need to loop through all of them and display each one. Although, in our case, each field can only have a single error, remember that we can add more than one validator to each field, so it's definitely possible to have forms which have several errors for each field. We don't want the user to have to fix one error and resubmit, only to find out that there are still others—instead, the user would want to be informed of all errors after a single submission of the form.

Modify the registration form in `home.html` to read as follows:

```
<div class="form-group">
  <div class="col-sm-9">
    {% if registrationform.email.errors %}
      <ul class="errors">{% for error in
      registrationform.email.errors %}<li>{{ error }}</li>
      {% endfor %}</ul>
    {% endif %}

    {{ registrationform.email(class="form-control",
    placeholder="Email Address" )}}
  </div>
</div>
<div class="form-group">
```

```
<div class="col-sm-9">
  {% if registrationform.password.errors %}
    <ul class="errors">{% for error in
    registrationform.password.errors %}<li>
    {{ error }}</li>{% endfor %}</ul>
  {% endif %}

  {{ registrationform.password(class="form-control",
  placeholder="Password" )}}
</div>
</div>
<div class="form-group">
  <div class="col-sm-9">
    {% if registrationform.password2.errors %}
      <ul class="errors">{% for error in
      registrationform.password2.errors %}<li>
      {{ error }}</li>{% endfor %}</ul>
    {% endif %}

    {{ registrationform.password2(class="form-control",
    placeholder="Confirm Password" )}}
  </div>
</div>
```

Note that we display our errors by building a list (within the `<ul>` tags), and that we assign these lists the class attribute of `errors`. We don't have any CSS code yet to define what error lists should look like, so let's fix that quickly.

Adding CSS for the errors

The CSS code for the errors is the only custom CSS code we'll be using in the project (the rest of our CSS is all free with Bootstrap). Therefore, it's fine to add our CSS directly into the `base.html` template file (we'll use it in our other templates as well), instead of creating a new external CSS file or editing the Bootstrap files.

If you're curious, take a look at the `bootstrap.min.css` file inside the `static/css` directory and note that it's quite difficult to read and modify (it's all in a single line!). The reason for this is to make the page load faster—every space and newline character makes the file a little bit bigger, which means our users' browsers would take longer to download the CSS file that is needed to display the web page. This is why large CSS and JavaScript libraries (such as the Bootstrap ones) come with a *minified* version (this is what the 'min' in `bootstrap.min.css` stands for). If we wanted to add our new CSS code to the Bootstrap file, we'd probably add it to the non-minified version and then re-minify it to create the minified one that we'd use in production.

Add the following style between the `<head>` tags of the `base.html` file:

```
<style type="text/css">
  ul.errors {
    list-style-type: none;
    padding: 0;
    color: red;
  }
</style>
```

The first line in the preceding styling code means that it should only apply to `<ul>` elements which have a class of errors (that is, the feedback messages we just added to our home page). The next three lines remove the bullet point that lists use by default, remove the indent that lists use by default, and set the font color to red.

Testing the final registration form

Our registration form is now finished. It now uses WTForms, so it is cleaner and easier to maintain, and we don't have to rely on a developer knowing that the HTML `name` attribute has to match up with the Python code. Let's have a look to make sure everything still works and that our new error messages are displayed when we expect them to be and are not shown when we don't want them.

Run your application again and try to register a new account. Try out various combinations of errors, such as using an already registered e-mail address (remember that our test database is cleared every time we restart the application), using a password that is too short, using non-matching strings for the two `password` fields, or using an invalid e-mail address. If all has gone according to plan, your form with errors should look similar to the one below:

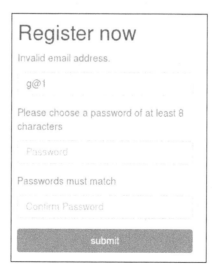

There are a couple of interesting things to note about the last image. First, note that the e-mail address g@1 is taken to be valid by the HTML5 input box (frontend validation), but not by the Email() validator (backend validation). This is why I could submit the form even though I'm using a browser that supports the HTML5 e-mail field, and was only told that the e-mail address was invalid after the data went to the backend. Second, note that after the form was submitted, the e-mail address was repopulated automatically, while the password fields are now blank. This is a useful default of most browsers. We are likely to want to submit similar information the second time round, after fixing the errors, but for security reasons, we always want to get rid of passwords as quickly as possible.

Note the '**Invalid email address**.' message in the preceding image. In our forms.py file, we only specified the error message for the case when the password was too short, but WTForms provides default messages for its built-in validators. Similarly, if you leave the password field blank, you'll see the message '**This field is required**' — another useful default that we did not have to write.

That's most of the heavy lifting done for form validation and user feedback. Now that you have a good conceptual grasp of how everything works, we'll go over it quickly once:

- Displaying feedback when the user's registration is successful (at the moment, we rather pessimistically only seem to be confirmed with failure, but the user will want to know that an account has been successfully registered if everything goes well).

- Moving our login form to WTForms and adding feedback for when users fail to log in.

- Moving our 'new table' form to WTForms and adding feedback where necessary.

Adding a successful registration notification

Normally, we would show the user a new page after a successful registration, thanking them for registering and informing them that everything has been successful (see the next chapter for a more complete list of things we could improve on if we were writing this application for a production environment instead of using it as an educational project). To keep our application to as few pages as possible, and to prevent this book from growing too long, we'll show the user a JavaScript popup box instead. Generally, when creating user interfaces, we want to avoid as many popups as possible, as users find them irritating. However, they are occasionally necessary, so using one here will help keep our application simple and give us an opportunity to learn a bit more JavaScript.

JavaScript is event-based. This means that we can write code that is triggered by user actions (such as a mouse click) or other events such as an `'onload'` event, which is triggered when a specific resource loads in the user's browser. Previously, in our Crime Map project, we used this to initialize the JavaScript Google Map widget after the `<body>` tag had loaded. Now we'll do something similar, but use this to display a JavaScript alert box instead. We'll also make our message dynamic and pass it to the frontend from the backend code.

Passing the message from the application code

The backend change for this is easy. Simply change the `register()` function to pass in the appropriate message if we process all the input data without any errors. In `waitercaller.py`, update the `register()` function to read as follows:

```
hashed = PH.get_hash(form.password2.data + salt)
DB.add_user(form.email.data, salt, hashed)
return render_template("home.html", registrationform=form,
onloadmessage="Registration successful. Please log in.")

return render_template("home.html", registrationform=form)
```

Using the message in the template code

The change is slightly trickier to implement in our template because we don't actually have access to the `<body>` tag (where we want to specify the JavaScript alert) in our `home.html` template. Instead, our `<body>` is defined in our `base.html` skeleton template from which all our other templates inherit.

To modify the `<body>` tag only in our `home.html` template, we need to make the `<body>` tag appear within an inheritable Jinja block, similar to our content block. To do this, we need to make changes to our `base.html` template and to our `home.html` template.

In `base.html`, make the following change where the `<body>` tag is created:

```
</head>
{% block bodytag %}

<body>
{% endblock %}
```

Now the `<body>` tag can be overwritten by child templates, as it appears inside a configurable block. In `home.html`, we'll overwrite the `<body>` block directly after the first line, if an alert message is specified. Remember that if this message is not specified, the `home.html` template will simply inherit the default `<body>` tag from the `base.html` template. In `home.html`, add the following code directly after the first line:

```
{% block bodytag %}
  <body {% if onloadmessage %} onload="alert('{{onloadmessage}}');" {%
  endif %}>
{% endblock %}
```

The only slightly tricky part is matching up all the quotation marks and brackets in the `onload` attribute. The entire `alert` function (the JavaScript we want to run) should appear within double quotation marks. The string inside the `alert` function (the message that is actually displayed to the user) should be inside single quotation marks. Finally, the `onloadmessage` variable should be inside double braces, so that we get the contents of the variable rather than the string of the variable name.

Now, after a successful registration, the user will see an alert confirming that everything went well and that a login is possible, as seen in the following image. It would be better to add a new page to properly inform the user of the successful registration, but to keep our app simple (and so we could introduce the onload functionality, which is generally useful), we opted for a slightly messier way of communicating this.

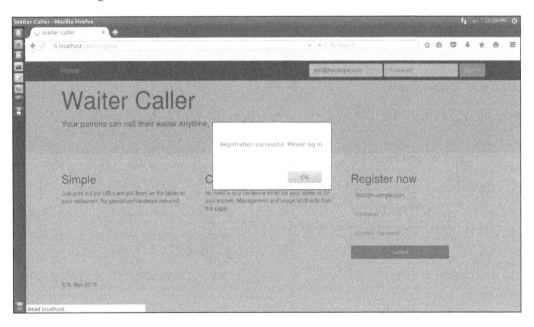

Modifying the login form

The changes necessary to move the login form to WTForms are very similar to the changes we made for the registration form, so we'll provide the code with minimal discussion. Refer to the code bundle if you are unsure where to insert the code or make changes.

Creating the new LoginForm in the application code

In forms.py, add the LoginForm class:

```
class LoginForm(Form):
    loginemail = EmailField('email',
    validators=[validators.DataRequired(), validators.Email()])
    loginpassword = PasswordField('password',
    validators=[validators.
    DataRequired(message="Password field is required")])
    submit = SubmitField('submit', [validators.DataRequired()])
```

Here we specify a custom message for the password field's DataRequired validator, as the error messages won't align with the fields as nicely as they did for the registration form. We also use the variable names loginemail and loginpassword, as these will become the HTML element id and name attributes, and it's preferable that they don't get overridden by the login and password fields in the registration form on the same page.

In waitercaller.py, add the import for the login form:

```
from forms import LoginForm
```

And rewrite the login() function as follows:

```
@app.route("/login", methods=["POST"])
def login():
    form = LoginForm(request.form)
    if form.validate():
        stored_user = DB.get_user(form.loginemail.data)
        if stored_user and
        PH.validate_password(form.loginpassword.data,
        stored_user['salt'], stored_user['hashed']):
            user = User(form.loginemail.data)
            login_user(user, remember=True)
            return redirect(url_for('account'))
        form.loginemail.errors.append("Email or password invalid")
    return render_template("home.html", loginform=form,
    registrationform=RegistrationForm())
```

It may seem that the "**Email or password invalid**" error is quite vague and could be more specific. It's true that the user may find it helpful to know where the mistake lies, as many people use many different e-mail addresses and different passwords. Thus, it would be convenient to know whether you, as a user, have entered the wrong e-mail and need to try to remember which e-mail address you signed up for, or if you have the correct e-mail address and have misremembered your anniversary or date of birth or whatever mnemonic you use to remember your password. However, the convenience is offset by yet another security issue. If we display "**Invalid password**" when the user enters a correct e-mail address but the incorrect password, this would allow a malicious attacker to try a large list of e-mail addresses against our website, and slowly build up a list of e-mail addresses that belong to our users. The attacker could then target these users in a phishing attack by using the knowledge that these users are our customers. This is yet another case that shows how developers have to be constantly vigilant against what information they might be allowing an attacker to infer, even if it's not directly provided.

The last backend changes that we need to make are to initialize and pass in a new `LoginForm` object whenever we render the `home.html` template. These changes have to be made:

- Once in the `home()` function
- Three times in the `register()` function

Change the `home()` function to read as follows:

```
@app.route("/")
def home():
  return render_template("home.html",
  loginform=LoginForm(), registrationform=RegistrationForm())
```

Change the last two lines of the `register()` function to:

```
    return render_template("home.html", loginform=LoginForm(),
    registrationform=form, onloadmessage="Registration successful.
    Please log in.")
    return render_template("home.html", loginform=LoginForm(),
    registrationform=form)
```

And the `return` statement in the middle of the `register()` function to:

```
    return render_template("home.html", loginform=LoginForm(),
    registrationform=form)
```

Using the new LoginForm in the template

For the template changes, `home.html` should now use the following `login` form:

```
<form class="navbar-form navbar-right" action="/login"
method="POST">
  {% if loginform.errors %}
    <ul class="errors">
      {% for field_name, field_errors in loginform.errors|dictsort
      if field_errors %}
        {% for error in field_errors %}
          <li>{{ error }}</li>
        {% endfor %}
      {% endfor %}
    </ul>
  {% endif %}
  {{ loginform.csrf_token}}
  <div class="form-group">
    {{ loginform.email(class="form-control", placeholder="Email
    Address")}}
  </div>
  <div class="form-group">
    {{ loginform.password(class="form-control",
    placeholder="Password")}}
  </div>
  <div class="form-group">
    {{ loginform.submit(value="Sign in",
    class="btn btn-success")}}
  </div>
</form>
```

Instead of displaying the errors above each field, as we did for the registration form, we'll just display all the errors above the login form. To do this, we can use the `loginform.errors` property, which is a dictionary mapping of each field to a list of its errors. The error displaying code is therefore slightly more verbose, as it has to loop through all the keys and values of this dictionary, and we use the convenient `|dictsort` Jinja notation to sort the dictionary before displaying the errors.

Modifying the create table form

The last form change we need to make is to the create table form, for when an already logged-in user adds a new restaurant table to his or her account. The new form to be added to `forms.py` looks like this:

```
class CreateTableForm(Form):
  tablenumber = TextField('tablenumber',
    validators=[validators.DataRequired()])
  submit = SubmitField('createtablesubmit',
    validators=[validators.DataRequired()])
```

This requires a new import in `forms.py` as well:

```
from wtforms import TextField
```

In `waitercaller.py`, we need to import the new form with:

```
from forms import CreateTableForm
```

Update the `account_createtable()` function to:

```
@app.route("/account/createtable", methods=["POST"])
@login_required
def account_createtable():
  form = CreateTableForm(request.form)
  if form.validate():
    tableid = DB.add_table(form.tablenumber.data,
      current_user.get_id())
    new_url = BH.shorten_url(config.base_url + "newrequest/" +
      tableid)
    DB.update_table(tableid, new_url)
    return redirect(url_for('account'))

  return render_template("account.html", createtableform=form,
    tables=DB.get_tables(current_user.get_id()))
```

And the `account()` route to:

```
@app.route("/account")
@login_required
def account():
    tables = DB.get_tables(current_user.get_id())
    return render_template("account.html",
      createtableform=CreateTableForm(), tables=tables)
```

Finally, the form in the `account.html` template should be changed to:

```
<form class="form-inline" action="/account/createtable"
method="POST">
  <div class="form-group">
    {% if createtableform.tablenumber.errors %}
      <ul class="errors">
        {% for error in createtableform.tablenumber.errors %}
          <li>{{error}}</li>
        {% endfor %}
      </ul>
    {% endif %}
    {{ createtableform.csrf_token}}
    {{ createtableform.tablenumber(class="form-control",
      placeholder="Table number or name")}}
    {{ createtableform.submit(value="Create",
      class="btn btn-primary") }}
  </div>
</form>
```

At the moment, if the user leaves the field blank and hits the **Create** button, we can only ever have a single error displayed on the `create table` form, that is, '**This field is required**', which we can see in the following screenshot:

With this in mind, it is debatable whether the for loop should loop through all the error messages. On the one hand, it is bad to 'future proof' too much, as you are left with a code base that contains a lot of unnecessary code that is over complicated. On the other hand, we may well add more error messages to the WTForm (such as if the user tries to create a table with a number that already exists), and therefore, it is arguably worthwhile to add the for loop.

The one form left that we have not converted to WTForms is the `delete table` form. As this is only a single **Submit** button, it is left as an exercise (the CSRF protection would still be a worthwhile gain in moving this form to WTForms.).

Summary

We've fleshed out our application's functionality, and it's now a lot more powerful. We added **Dashboard** and **Account** pages, and wrote all the application code, database code, and frontend code to handle our requirements.

We looked at Jinja templates as a way to avoid duplicating the frontend code, and we also looked at how to use the bitly API to shorten links.

We then added WTForms, and saw how this could make our user feedback easier, our forms easier to validate, and our web application more secure. Our users are now kept up-to-date with information about their registration, login, and usage of the application.

In the next chapter, we'll add a real database to our code and then work on some finishing touches.

11
Using MongoDB with Our Waiter Caller Project

Our web application now has nearly all of its functionality. If we plan to monetize this application, now would be the time where we'd demo it to potential customers. Even though their data (such as their account name and virtual table data) would be lost every time we had to restart our server, this data is trivial enough to make a full demo of the application feasible.

In this chapter, we will add a proper database for use in production. We'll use MongoDB—a slightly controversial NoSQL database management system that has become extremely popular, arguably largely because of its simplicity. We'll take a look at how to install in on our VPS, configure it correctly, and access it using a Python driver. Then, we'll implement the full `DBHelper` class to replace `MockDBHelper`, which we use for testing. To end off, we'll look at adding indices to MongoDB and a favicon to our application.

In this chapter, we'll cover the following topics:

- Introducing MongoDB
- Installing MongoDB
- Using the MongoDB shell
- Introducing PyMongo
- Adding some finishing touches

Introducing MongoDB

MongoDB is a NoSQL database. This means that unlike the MySQL database we used for our Crime Map project, it is not organized into tables, rows, and columns; instead, it is organized into collections, documents, and fields. While it can be useful to think of these new terms as a sort of translation from those we use for relational databases, the concepts do not perfectly translate. If you have a background in relational databases, a useful and more complete reference to these translations can be found on the official MongoDB website at `https://docs.mongodb.org/manual/reference/sql-comparison/`.

MongoDB's structure is much more flexible than that of a SQL database — not all of our data has to confirm to a specific schema, and this can save development time. For our Crime Map project, we had to spend time up front looking at our data and deciding how to represent it in a database. We then had to set up a bunch of fields, specifying the data type, length, and other constraints. MongoDB, by contrast, requires none of this. It's more flexible than an RDBMS, and it uses documents to represent the data. Documents are essentially bits of JSON data similar to the data we pulled from the APIs we used. This means that we can easily add or remove fields as necessary, and we do not need to specify data types for our fields.

The downside of this is that by not being forced to be structured and consistent, it's easy for us to get lazy and fall into bad practices of mixing different data types in a single field and allowing invalid data to pollute our database. In short, MongoDB gives us more freedom, but in doing so, it shifts some of the responsibility for being clean and consistent onto our shoulders.

Installing MongoDB

MongoDB can be found in the Ubuntu software repositories, but as updates are frequent and the repository versions tend to lag behind, it's highly recommended to install it from the official Mongo package directly.

We'll go through how to do this step by step here, but as the installation procedures may change, it's advisable to get an updated version of the required URLs and steps from the official installation guide available at `https://docs.mongodb.org/manual/tutorial/install-mongodb-on-ubuntu/`.

The first thing we need to do is import MongoDB's public key so that the installation can be authenticated. On your VPS only (as before, we will not install a database server on our development machine), run the following:

```
sudo apt-key adv --keyserver hkp://keyserver.ubuntu.com:80
--recv EA312927
```

Now that we have the key, we can use the following command to add a link to the MongoDB package to our software sources. Note that this command is specific to Ubuntu 14.04 "Trusty", which, at the time of writing, is the latest long-term support Ubuntu version. If your VPS runs a different version of Ubuntu, make sure you get the correct command from the MongoDB documentation link provided earlier. To discover which version of Ubuntu you have, run `lsb_release -a` in your terminal and examine the output for a version number and name:

```
echo "deb http://repo.mongodb.org/apt/ubuntu trusty/mongodb-org/3.2
multiverse" | sudo tee /etc/apt/sources.list.d/mongodb-org-3.2.list
```

Now, we simply need to update our source lists by running:

```
sudo apt-get update
```

Finally, do the actual installation by running the following command:

```
sudo apt-get install -y mongodb-org
```

The preceding command will install MongoDB with some sensible defaults and start the server. It'll also configure it in such a way that the server will start up automatically if you reboot your VPS.

Using the MongoDB shell

Similarly to what we discussed with MySQL, MongoDB comes with a simple shell. This is ideal to run quick, one-off commands and get used to the syntax. Let's run through the basic CRUD operations to get familiar with how MongoDB works.

As in our previous project, once we introduce MongoDB, we'll move to using it only through Python code; however, to start out, we'll write commands directly in the shell. This means there will be some slight differences in syntax, but as nearly everything is JSON based, these differences shouldn't be a problem.

Starting the MongoDB shell

To start the MongoDB shell, run the following command on your VPS:

```
mongo
```

This will start the interactive MongoDB shell as in the following image, which you can exit at any time by pressing *Ctrl + C* or by typing `exit` into the shell and pressing *Enter*.

Running commands in the MongoDB shell

As with MySQL, the top-level concept in MongoDB is a database. By default, this will connect to a database named `test`. We can change databases using the `use` command. Run the following command in the shell:

```
use sandbox
```

You should see the output "**Switched to db sandbox**". This is where we can note the first big difference between MySQL and MongoDB. With MySQL, we would first have had to create the database. This is a common pattern we'll see with MongoDB; if you reference a database, collection, or field that doesn't exist, it'll be automatically created for you.

Creating data with MongoDB

Now, let's create a collection (similar to a table in our MySQL database from the Crime Map project) and add a document (as with a row from a table in our MySQL database) to it. Run the following in the MongoDB shell:

```
db.people.insert({"name":"John Smith", "age": 35})
```

In the preceding command, `db` refers to the current database. Directly after, `people` refers to the collection called of this name. As it doesn't exist, it'll get created as we attempt to use it. Following this is `insert`, which means we want to add something to the database. We will pass as an argument (inside round the brackets), which is a JSON structure. In our case, we represented a person with a JSON object containing the person's name and age. Note that everything is in quotation marks except for the value of the `age` field; again, unlike MySQL, we don't have to specify the types for this data. MongoDB will store the name as a string and the age as an integer, but it applies no restrictions to these fields.

Add another person to the database to make the next operations that we will try out more meaningful. Run the following:

```
db.people.insert({"name":"Mary Jones"})
```

Reading data with MongoDB

Instead of the SQL concept of a `SELECT` statement, MongoDB uses a `find()` command. Similarly to SQL, we can specify the criteria to search for in data and also choose which fields we want the database to return. Run the following command:

```
db.people.find()
```

This is the most basic version of the `find` operation. It'll simply *find* or *retrieve* all the data and all its fields from the `people` collection. You should see MongoDB output all the information about both the people we just added. You'll note that each person also has an `ObjectId` field added; MongoDB adds unique identifier fields to each of our documents automatically, and these `ID` fields are also automatically indexed.

We can also use `find` with a single argument. The argument specifies criteria, and MongoDB only returns documents that match. Run the following command:

```
db.people.find({"name":"John Smith"})
```

This will return all the fields from all the records if the name matches `John Smith`, so you should see a single result returned and printed to the shell, as in the screenshot that follows:

```
> db.people.find({"name":"John Smith"})
{ "_id" : ObjectId("56d5e9a1bf738a9a34175181"), "name" : "Jo
hn Smith", "age" : 35 }
>
```

Finally, if we don't want all the fields returned, we can run the `find` command and pass in a second argument to specify which fields we want. Run the following command, and you should see results as in the following screenshot:

```
db.people.find({"name":"John Smith"}, {"age":1})
```

```
> db.people.find({"name":"John Smith"}, {"age":1})
{ "_id" : ObjectId("56d5e9a1bf738a9a34175181"), "age" : 35 }
> _
```

The first argument says we're only interested in people who are called "John Smith". The second argument says we're only interested in their age. Here, 1 is a flag that says we want this field. We could instead use 0 to say that we're not interested in a field, in which case, all the fields will be returned except this one.

Note that even though we said we were only interested in the age field, the preceding command returned the _id field as well. The _id field is always returned unless explicitly excluded. For example, we could run the following:

```
db.people.find({"name":"John Smith"}, {"age":1, "_id": 0})
```

This will return only John's age and nothing else. Also, note that the key for the _id field is _id and not id; this is to prevent a conflict with the id keyword in many programming languages, including Python.

Each of our examples used very basic JSON objects with only a single value, but we can specify multiple values for each argument. Consider the difference between the following commands:

```
db.people.find({"name":"John Smith", "age":1})
db.people.find({"name":"John Smith"}, {"age":1})
```

The first command uses find with a single argument that returns all records for all the people with the name John Smith and aged 1. The second command uses find with two arguments and returns the age field (and _id field) of all the people with the name John Smith.

A final difference to note from MySQL is that there is no need to commit new data. Once we run the insert statement, the data will be in the database until we remove it.

Updating data with MongoDB

Updating existing records is slightly more complicated. MongoDB provides an update method, which can be called in the same way as insert and find. It also takes two arguments—the first specifying the criteria to find the document we want to update, and the second providing a new document to replace it with. Run the following command:

```
db.people.update({"name":"John Smith"},
{"name":"John Smith", "age":43})
```

This finds the person with the name John Smith, and replaces him with a new person, also with the name John Smith and aged 43. If there are a lot of fields and we only want to change a single one, it is tedious and wasteful to recreate all the old fields. Therefore, we can use MongoDB's $set keyword instead, which will only replace the specified fields inside a document instead of replacing the whole document. Run the following command:

```
db.people.update({"name":"John Smith"}, {$set: {"age":35}})
```

This updates John's age back to 35 again, which is probably a relief to him. Instead of having to overwrite the whole document, here we only changed the age field. We did this using the $set keyword in the second argument. Note that the update function still takes two arguments and the second one now has a nested JSON structure — the out JSON object has $set as the key and another JSON object as a value. The inner JSON object specifies the updates that we want to make.

Deleting data with MongoDB

Deleting data is as easy as finding it. We will simply use the remove function instead of find and then specify the matching criteria in a single argument, just as we would with find. Run the following command to delete John from our database:

```
db.people.remove({"name":"John Smith"})
```

You will see a confirmation that one record was deleted, as shown in the following image:

```
> db.people.remove({"name":"John Smith"})
WriteResult({ "nRemoved" : 1 })
>
```

You can also check that John is deleted by running the following:

```
db.people.find()
```

Now, only Mary will be returned, as in the following image:

```
> db.people.find()
{ "_id" : ObjectId("56d5ec656167126b1233848c"), "name" : "Ma
ry Jones" }
>
```

To remove all the documents from a collection, we can pass in an empty argument. Run the following command to remove all the remaining people:

```
db.people.remove({})
```

Here, {} specifies an empty criteria condition and therefore matches all the documents. Check that our `people` collection is empty by running the `find` command again, as follows:

```
db.people.find()
```

You'll see no output, as shown in the following screenshot (with the earlier examples included for context), because our `people` collection is now empty:

```
> db.people.remove({"name":"John Smith"})
WriteResult({ "nRemoved" : 1 })
> db.people.find()
{ "_id" : ObjectId("56d5ec656167126b1233848c"), "name" : "Ma
ry Jones" }
> db.people.remove({})
WriteResult({ "nRemoved" : 1 })
> db.people.find()
> _
```

Now that we looked at the basics of MongoDB, let's take a look at how to run similar commands using Python instead of operating through the shell.

Introducing PyMongo

PyMongo is a library that implements drivers for MongoDB and will allow us to execute commands on our database from our application code. As usual, install it through pip using the following command (note that, similarly to MongoDB, you only need to install this library on the server):

```
pip install --user pymongo
```

Now, we can import this library into our application and build our real `DBHelper` class, implementing all the methods we used in our `MockDBHelper` class.

Writing the DBHelper class

The last class that we need is the `DBHelper` class, which will contain all the functions that are required for our application code to talk to our database. This class will use the `pymongo` library we just installed in order to run MongoDB commands. Create a file named `dbhelper.py` in the `waiter` directory and add the following code:

```
import pymongo

DATABASE = "waitercaller"
```

```
class DBHelper:

  def __init__(self):
    client = pymongo.MongoClient()
    self.db = client[DATABASE]
```

This code imports the `pymongo` library, and in the constructor, it creates a client—a Python object that will let us run the CRUD operations we tried out earlier on our database. We defined the name of our database as a global one, and in the second line of our constructor, we connected to the specified database using `client`.

Adding the user methods

For user management, we need the same two functions we had in our mock class. The first is to get a user out of the database (in order to log this user in) and the second is to add new users to the database (in order to register new users). Add the following two methods to the `DBHelper` class:

```
def get_user(self, email):
    return self.db.users.find_one({"email": email})

def add_user(self, email, salt, hashed):
    self.db.users.insert({"email": email, "salt": salt,
    "hashed": hashed})
```

For the first method, we used PyMongo's `find_one()` function. This is similar to the `find()` method we used in the MongoDB shell but returns only a single match instead of all the matching results. As we only allow one registration per e-mail address, there will always be either one or zero matches. Using `find()` instead of `find_one()` here would also work, but we would get back a Python generator that produces a single or zero element. Using `find_one()`, we will get back either a single user result or none, which is exactly what our login code needs.

For the `add_user()` method, we used `insert()` exactly as we discussed when playing with the MongoDB shell and inserted a new document containing the e-mail address, salt, and salted hash of the password.

Adding the table methods

We need methods to handle the following cases for the virtual tables that our users will create:

* One to add new tables
* One to update tables (so that we can add the shortened bitly URL)

- One to get all the tables (so that we can display them in the **Account** page)
- One to get a single table (so that we can add the local table number to our requests)
- One to delete a table

This is a nice set of methods as it demonstrates all four of the CRUD database operations. Add the following code to the DBHelper class:

```
def add_table(self, number, owner):
    new_id = self.db.tables.insert({"number": number, "owner":
    owner})
    return new_id

def update_table(self, _id, url):
    self.db.tables.update({"_id": _id}, {"$set": {"url": url}})

def get_tables(self, owner_id):
    return list(self.db.tables.find({"owner": owner_id}))

def get_table(self, table_id):
    return self.db.tables.find_one({"_id": ObjectId(table_id)})

def delete_table(self, table_id):
    self.db.tables.remove({"_id": ObjectId(table_id)})
```

For the add_table() method, MongoDB will assign a unique identifier every time we insert a table. This gives us true multiuser support. Our mock code used the user-chosen table number as a unique identifier and would break with multiple users when two or more users chose the same table number. In the add_table() method, we returned this unique identifier to the application code, which can then be used to build the URL that's needed to make new requests for this specific table.

The update_table() method uses the insert() function that we discussed earlier. As in our previous example, we used the $set keyword to keep our original data intact, and only edited a specific field (instead of overwriting the entire document).

 Note that unlike in the MongoDB shell example, we now need quotation marks around $set; this makes it syntactically legal Python code (all the keys of a dictionary have to be strings), and PyMongo takes care of the magic in the background to convert our Python dictionaries into MongoDB commands and objects.

The `get_tables()` function used the `find()` function instead of the `find_one()` function that we used for the user code. This caused PyMongo to return a Python generator that can produce all the data that matched the *find* criteria. As we assumed that we'll always be able to load all the tables into memory, we converted this generator to a list, which we then passed to our template.

The `get_table()` function is used in cases when we only have access to the table ID and need to get other information about the table. This is exactly the scenario when we processed requests; the URL of the request contained the table's unique ID but wanted to add the table number to the **Dashboard** page. The unique identifiers that MongoDB generated are actually objects rather than simple strings, but we had just the string from our URL. Therefore, we created `ObjectId` and passed in the string before using this ID to query the database. `ObjectId` can be imported from the `bson` library, which was installed automatically. This means we also need to add another import statement. Add the following line to the top of the `dbhelper.py` file:

```
from bson.objectid import ObjectId
```

Finally, the `delete_table()` method used the `remove()` function exactly as we did before. Here, we removed a table by its unique identifier, so again, we created an `ObjectId` object from the string we had before passing it to the database.

Adding the request methods

We have to add the last three methods to the `DBHelper` class to deal with the attention requests. We need to:

- Add a request when a patron visits the provided URL
- Get all the requests for a specific user to display on the **Dashboard** page
- Delete requests from the database when the user hits the **Resolve** button

Add the following methods to the `dbhelper.py` file:

```
    def add_request(self, table_id, time):
        table = self.get_table(table_id)
        self.db.requests.insert({"owner": table['owner'],
        "table_number": table['number'],
        "table_id": table_id, "time": time})

    def get_requests(self, owner_id):
        return list(self.db.requests.find({"owner": owner_id}))

    def delete_request(self, request_id):
        self.db.requests.remove({"_id": ObjectId(request_id)})
```

Changing the application code

Now that we have a real `DBHelper` class, we need to conditionally import it based on which environment we're in. Change the import for the `MockDBHelper` class in the `waitercaller.py` file to read, as follows:

```
if config.test
    from mockdbhelper import MockDBHelper as DBHelper
else:
    from dbhelper import DBHelper
```

Ensure that the preceding four lines are added beneath the `config` import.

Also, our `DBHelper` class deals mainly with many instances of `ObjectId`, while our `MockDBHelper` class uses strings. We therefore need a small change to our `account_createtable()` function to cast `ObjectId` to a string. Take a look at the line in `waitercaller.py` that reads the following:

```
new_url = BH.shorten_url(config.base_url +
"newrequest/" + tableid)
```

Now, change this to the following:

```
new_url = BH.shorten_url(config.base_url +
"newrequest/" + str(tableid))
```

This will ensure that `tableid` is always a string before we concatenate it to our URL.

The last code changes we need for our production is a different `config` file to specify the correct `base_url` for our VPS and to indicate that the `MockDBHelper` class should not be used. As we don't check our `config` file into our `git` repository, we'll need to create this directly on the VPS.

Testing our application in production

Our application should now be fully functional once we add the preceding code! As with the database section of our Crime Map application, this bit is the most delicate as we haven't been able to test the `DBHelper` code locally, and we'll have to debug it directly on the VPS. However, we're confident, from our `MockDBHelper` class, that all our application logic is working, and if the new database code holds up, everything else should go as expected. Let's push our code to the server and test it out.

Locally, run the following commands in your `waitercaller` directory:

```
git add .
git commit -m "DBHelper code"
git push origin master
```

On your VPS, change to the `WaiterCaller` directory, pull the new code, and restart Apache, as follows:

```
cd /var/www/waitercaller
git pull origin master
```

Now, create the production `config` file using nano by running the following command:

```
nano config.py
```

Type the following into the new `config.py` file, substituting the IP address in `base_url` with the IP address of your VPS.

```
test = False
base_url = "http://123.456.789.123/
```

Then, save and quit the file by hitting *Ctrl + X* and entering *Y* when prompted.

Now, run the following command to reload Apache with the new code:

```
sudo service apache2 reload
```

Visit the IP address of your VPS in your local browser and do a run-through of all the functionality to make sure everything works as expected. This includes attempting to sign up with invalid data, signing up, attempting to log in with invalid data, logging in, creating a table, creating a request, viewing the dashboard, waiting for the dashboard to refresh, resolving a request, and more. For a full test, all the actions should be completed several times in varying combinations.

You'll probably understand how tedious this gets even for our relatively simple application. For more complicated applications, it is well worth the effort to create automatic tests—code that imitates what a user would do on the site but also has built-in expectations of what should happen at each step. Tools such as Selenium (`www.seleniumhq.org`) come in very useful to build such tests.

 As always, if anything goes wrong or you get the dreaded "500: Internal Server Error", check the Apache error file at `/etc/log/apache2/error.log` for hints.

Adding some finishing touches

To end off, we'll add a couple of indices to our database to improve efficiency and prevent multiple requests from being open for a single table. After this, we'll add a favicon to personalize our web application.

Adding indices to MongoDB

Database indices are used to increase efficiency. Normally, to find a subset of documents in our database that match certain criteria (that is, whenever we use the MongoDB `find()` method), the database engine has to examine each record and add the ones that match the returned result. If we add an index to a specific field, the database will store more metadata, which can be thought about as storing a sorted copy of this field. To find out whether `john@example.com` appears in a sorted list is much more efficient than checking whether it appears in an unsorted list. However, the indices do take up additional storage space, so choosing where to add indices is a classic *space-time tradeoff* that's seen everywhere in computer science. MongoDB can also use indices to place some constraints on a field. In our case, we'll use a *unique* index, which prevents a new document from being added to the database if the value for the indexed field already appears in another document in this collection.

We'll add two indices to MongoDB. We'll add an index on the `email` field of our `users` collection as we will use this field to find users on login, and we want the lookups to be as fast as possible. We also want to ensure at a database level that each e-mail address is unique. We already have two checks for this: the HTML5 field does a frontend check, and our application code does a backend check. Even though a database check may seem unnecessary, it takes little effort to set up and follows the good principles of baked-in security (in which checks aren't just tacked on as an afterthought, but all data is validated as often as possible instead), and the principle that each *layer* of an application (the frontend, application layer, and database layer in our case) shouldn't blindly trust the data that is passed from a higher layer.

We'll also add a unique index on the `table_id` field for a requests collection. This will prevent a single impatient table from spamming the dashboard with multiple requests by refreshing the page that creates a new request. It's also useful because our requests are created using GET requests, which can easily be duplicated (by a browser preloading a page or a social network scraping the links a user visits to find out more about them). By ensuring that each request's `table_id` is unique, we can prevent both of these issues.

Where do we add indices?

When we built our MySQL database, we had a setup script that ran independently of our Crime Map web application. This setup script built the skeleton of the database, and we wrote it in Python so that we could easily run it again if we ever needed to migrate to a new server or to reinstall our database.

As MongoDB is so much more flexible, we didn't need a setup script. We can start our application off on a new server, and — as long as we install MongoDB — the database will recreate itself from scratch as new data is added or the old data is restored from a backup.

The lack of a setup script does mean that we don't really have a good place to add indices to our database. If we add the indices through the MongoDB shell, it means that someone has to remember to add them again if the application needs to migrate to a new server. Therefore, we'll create an independent Python script just to make the indices. On your local machine, create a Python file in the `waitercaller` directory and call it `create_mongo_indices.py`. Add the following code:

```
import pymongo
client = pymongo.MongoClient()
c = client['waitercaller']
print c.users.create_index("email", unique=True)
print c.requests.create_index("table_id", unique=True)
```

The connection code is the same that we used before, and the code used to create indices is simple enough. We called the `create_index()` method on the collection we want to create an index on and then passed in the field name to use to create the index. In our case, we also passed in the `unique=True` flag to specify that the indices should also have a unique constraint added to them.

Now, we need to make a small change to our application so that it can deal with the case of a new request being made when an identical request is already open. In the `dbhelper.py` file, update the `add_request()` method to the following:

```
def add_request(self, table_id, time):
    table = self.get_table(table_id)
    try:
        self.db.requests.insert({"owner": table['owner'],
        "table_number": table['number'], "table_id": table_id,
        "time": time})
        return True
    except pymongo.errors.DuplicateKeyError:
        return False
```

If we try to insert a request into our database with a duplicate `table_id` field, `DuplicateKeyError` will be thrown. In the updated code, we will catch this error and return `False` to indicate that the request wasn't successfully created. We will also now return `True` when the request is successful. To take advantage of this information in the application code, we also need to update the `new_request()` method. Edit the method so that it looks similar to this:

```
@app.route("/newrequest/<tid>")
def new_request(tid):
    if DB.add_request(tid, datetime.datetime.now()):
        return "Your request has been logged and a waiter will
        be with you shortly"
    return "There is already a request pending for this table.
    Please be patient, a waiter will be there ASAP"
```

Now, we will check whether the new request was successfully created or whether an existing one blocked it. In the latter case, we will return a different message, requesting patience from the patron.

To test the new functionality, add the new and modified files to Git (`waitercaller.py`, `dbhelper.py`, `create_mongo_indices.py`), commit, and then push them. On your VPS, pull in the new changes, restart Apache, and run the following:

```
python create_mongo_indices.py
```

To create the indices we discussed before, run some tests again in your browser to make sure nothing broke and to verify that you get the new message displayed when you visit the same attention request URL repeatedly without resolving the request, as in the screenshot that follows:

You may find that, due to your browser pre-fetching pages, attention requests get made automatically when you first create tables through the account page. If you see the message as displayed in the above image when you don't expect to, resolve any open requests on the dashboard page, and visit the newrequest URL again.

Adding a favicon

The last thing we'll add to our application is a favicon. *Favicons* are the small images that most browsers display in the tab bar when a page is open and on the bookmarks bar if a user bookmarks a site. They add a friendly touch to the site and help a user identify a site more quickly.

The tricky part about favicons is that they have to be really small. It's customary to use a 16x16 pixel image as a favicon—which doesn't leave that much room for creativity. There are some nice websites to help you create the perfect favicon for your website. One such site is `favicon.cc`, which allows you to create a favicon from scratch (giving you 16x16 blank pixels to start), or it can import an image. Using the import functionality, you can use a bigger image that `favicon.cc` attempts to reduce to 16x16 pixels—this has mixed results and generally works better with simpler images. An example favicon is included in the code bundle in the static directory, and an enlarged version of it is shown in the following image:

Once you have an icon (you can use the one provided in the code bundle), it's easy to tell Flask to serve it along with the rest of the page. Make sure your icon is called `favicon.ico` (the standard extension for icon files is `.ico`) and put it in the `waitercaller/static` directory. Then, add the following line to the `<head>` section of the `base.html` template:

```
<link rel="shortcut icon" href="{{ url_for('static',
filename='favicon.ico') }}">
```

This creates a link to the `favicon.ico` file using Jinja's `url_for` function to generate the full URL needed to be directed to the static directory, which is simply converted to the plain HTML (which you can see by hitting **View source** in your browser). Take a look at the following:

```
<link rel="shortcut icon" href="/static/favicon.ico">
```

Now, if you reload the page again, you will see the favicon in the tab heading, and if you bookmark the page, you'll view the icon in the bookmarks toolbar of your browser as well, as seen in the following screenshot:

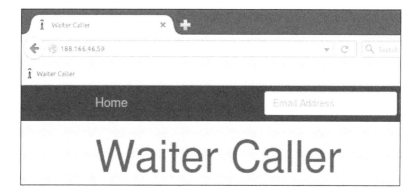

That's it for our last project. Of course, no web application is ever truly complete, and there are countless improvements to make and features to add. By this stage in the book, you will have more than enough knowledge to start adding your own changes and bringing your original ideas into creation, either as extensions to the projects we walked through in this book or from scratch, as brand-new web applications.

Summary

In this chapter, we completed our Waiter Caller web application. We installed MongoDB on our server, learned how to use it through the shell, and then installed PyMongo. Using PyMongo, we created a new database helper class to allow our application code to run operations on the new database.

Finally, we added a favicon to make our web application friendlier and more aesthetically pleasing to users.

In the next and final chapter, we'll take a look at what could still be added to our application to improve usability and security and end with some pointers on where to look next to continue learning about Flask and web development through Python.

A Sneak Peek into the Future

We covered quite a variety of topics in this book, and we walked through the building of three functional and useful web applications. However, books, by nature, are of a finite length, while the world of web development tends towards the infinite, so we couldn't add everything. In this final chapter, we'll take a whistle-stop tour around the technologies that we weren't able to cover in detail. We'll start with looking at technologies that could be used directly to expand or improve the projects we created in this book. Then, we'll look at some more advanced Flask features that we didn't need to use in our projects but which will almost certainly be useful in other projects. Finally, we'll have a brief discussion of the technologies that are useful for web development in general but are not specific to either the projects we built here or to Flask.

Expanding the projects

The projects we built are all functional, but they are not quite ready for heavy, real-time use. If they were to be built out to handle thousands of users or were commercial applications, they would need a few more features. These are discussed in the following sections.

Adding a domain name

We accessed all of our projects using the IP address of our VPS. You're almost certainly used to visiting web applications using domain names rather than IP addresses. When you use a domain name, such as `http://google.com`, your browser first sends off a request to a DNS server to find out what the IP address associated with this domain is. DNS servers are similar to huge automatic telephone books that exist solely to translate the domain names that humans find easier to remember (such as `http://google.com`) in than the IP addresses that organize the Internet (for example, 123.456.789.123).

To use a domain name instead of the IP address, you need to purchase one from a registrar. Often your **Internet Service Provider** (**ISP**) can assist you with purchasing a domain name (such as `yourname.com`). Domain names are normally fairly inexpensive, and you can get them for as little as a few dollars a year.

Once you purchase a domain name, you need to set up the DNS settings correctly. Most ISPs have an online control panel where you can do this yourself, but you may have to contact them to assist you. Your domain needs to point to your VPS. To do this, you create an "A" type DNS record that maps the domain to your IP.

Once your domain name points at your server, you can configure Apache to recognize it by using it instead of our `example.com` placeholder that we put in the Apache configuration files, such as `/etc/apache2/sites-available/waitercaller.conf`.

Changes to domain names also take a while to propagate — that is, the major DNS servers of the world need to be updated so that when someone visits your domain name, the DNS server can redirect them to your IP address. DNS propagation can take hours.

Adding HTTPS

You've probably noticed that banks, large corporations such as Google and Microsoft, and an ever-growing number of other companies, have their websites automatically redirect to an **HTTPS** version. The "S" stands for *secure*, so the full acronym becomes **Hyper Text Transport Protocol Secure**. Whenever you see HTTPS in your browser's navigation bar (normally with a green padlock next to it) it means that all traffic flowing between you and the server is encrypted. This prevents so-called *man in the middle attacks*, where a malicious person between you and the server can view or modify the content that you and the server exchange.

Until recently, this encryption was achieved by the site owner by purchasing an expensive certificate from **Certificate Authority** (**CA**). CA's job is to act as a trusted third party between you and the server, issuing a signed certificate to the owner of a site. This certificate can be used to set up an encrypted channel between the client and the server. Because of the prohibitive cost, HTTPS was only used where security was absolutely necessary (for example, in online banking) and by companies such as Google who could afford the high fees. With everyone beginning to realize that the trust-based model of World Wide Web is inherently flawed, HTTPS is becoming more and more popular even for small blogs and personal websites. Companies such as Let's Encrypt (`https://letsencrypt.org`) are now offering certificates for free and these certificates can easily be installed and configured to work with popular web servers, such as Apache.

For our final project, as we are handling sensitive data (specifically passwords), using HTTPS is a must for nontrivial usage of our application, and it's also desirable for our other two projects (HTTPS is always better than HTTP). Although the process of setting up certificates to work with your web server is far simpler now than it was a couple of years ago, a full walk-through of how to set up Apache2 to play with a CA certificate is beyond the scope of this book.

However, if you only take the time to learn about one of the technologies mentioned in this chapter, then it should be this one. Here is a link to a very simple Digital Ocean tutorial that shows you how to set up the certificate on Ubuntu 14.04 to work with Apache2 (the exact configuration we used in this book):

```
https://www.digitalocean.com/community/tutorials/how-to-secure-
apache-with-let-s-encrypt-on-ubuntu-14-04
```

E-mail confirmation for new registrations

You probably noted in our third project that our registration process was a little bit unusual. The normal way for new users to register on a site is as follows:

1. User fills out registration form and submits it.
2. Server saves the data in the database.
3. Server generates a unique and secure token and stores the token associated with the registration, which it marks as incomplete.
4. Server e-mails the token to the user in the form of a URL and requests that the user click on the URL to confirm the account.
5. User clicks on URL with the unique token.
6. Server finds an incomplete registration associated with this token and marks the registration as confirmed.

The preceding process is in order to prove that the user gave us a real e-mail address to which he or she has access. Of course, the user does not want to wait for someone to manually send an e-mail, so the confirmation e-mail has to be sent automatically. This leads to a few complications, including the need to set up a mail server and the fact that the automatic confirmation e-mail we send may well end up in the user's spam folder, leading to frustration all round. Another option is to use an *E-mail as a service* platform, such as Amazon's **Simple E-mail Service** (**SES**). However, these are not usually free.

Once the user has a confirmed e-mail account, we can also use it to allow the user to reset a forgotten password. Again, this would involve sending an automatic e-mail to users who wanted to reset their password. The e-mail would again contain a secure unique token in a URL that the user would click on to prove that he or she really did make the password reset request. We would then allow the user to type in a new password and update the database with the new (hashed and salted) password. Note that we can't and shouldn't send the user his or her own password because we store only the salted and hashed version of the password; we have no way of discovering the forgotten one.

The complete user account system with automatic e-mail confirmations and the "forgot your password" functionality is fairly complex. We could set it up using nothing but Python and Flask and an e-mail server, but in the next section, we'll also discuss some more Flask extensions that could make this process easier.

Google Analytics

If we run any of the web applications commercially, we'll probably be interested in how many people actually use them. This would help us in deciding how (and whether) to monetize our applications and provide other useful insights.

The most common way to achieve this is through Google Analytics. This is a service from Google to track not only how many people visit your site but also how long they spend on it, how they found it, their country, information about the device they use for web browsing, and many other insightful statistics. Google Analytics is free, and to get started with using it, you need to simply create an account on `https://analytics.google.com` (or use your existing Google account). After filling in some information about your site, you'll be given a short snippet of JavaScript. This JavaScript code contains a unique tracking ID assigned to your site. You need to add the JavaScript code to your site, and whenever anyone visits the site, the JavaScript code will be loaded into their web browser and will send information about them to Google, which will then use the unique ID to associate the information with you. On the Google Analytics dashboard, you can then see graphs of the number of visitors, the length of their visits, and many more pieces of information.

In the case of our waiter-caller project, we'd add the JavaScript at the end of the `base.html` file along with the Bootstrap JavaScript code.

Scalability

The best problem to have as a web application creator is having made an application that is too popular. If lots of people are visiting your application, it means that you created something good (and you can possible start charging people money for it). Our little VPS will not handle a lot of traffic. If thousands of people visit the site simultaneously, we'll run out of network bandwidth, processing capacity, memory, and disk space very quickly.

A complete discussion on creating scalable web applications would be a book all on its own. However, some of the steps we would need to take would be:

- **Run the database on a dedicated machine**: At the moment, we run our web server and database on the same physical machine. For a larger web application, the database would have its own dedicated machine so that heavy database use (for instance, many restaurant patrons creating new requests) wouldn't have a negative impact on the people who just wanted to browse our home page. Normally, the database machine would have lots of disk space and memory, while the machine running the web server would focus more on having high bandwidth availability and processing power.

- **Run a load balancer**: If we have a lot of visitors, one machine will not be able to keep up with the load no matter how big and powerful the machine is. We would therefore run several duplicate web server machines. The problem would then be to evenly distribute new visitors among all the different machines. To solve this, we would use something called a *load balancer*, which is responsible for nothing but accepting the initial request from the user (that is, when the user visits your homepage) and assigning this user to one of the replica web servers.

As we grow bigger, the situation would grow more and more complicated, and we would add replica database machines as well. A popular site requires full-time maintenance, often by a team of people, because hardware fails, malicious users exist, and updates (which are necessary to mitigate attacks by malicious users) tend to break the compatibility between software. On the bright side, if any web applications were to grow popular enough to warrant the preceding, the application would probably also generate enough revenue to make all the issues discussed an "SEP", or somebody else's problem. That is, we could hire a system's administrator, a database administrator, and a chief security officer, tell them to sort it out, and spend the rest of our days on ocean cruises. On this note, let's take a look at some Flask-specific expansions to our knowledge.

Expanding your Flask knowledge

You might expect that Flask, being a micro framework, could be covered in its entirety in a single book. However, there are some potentially very useful parts of Flask that we didn't need for any of our three projects. We'll briefly outline these here.

VirtualEnv

The first library worth mentioning is not actually Flask-specific, and if you've spent some time on Python development before, you will almost certainly come across it. `VirtualEnv` is a Python library that creates a virtual Python environment on your machine. It can be used in conjunction with Flask either only on your development machine or both on your development machine and server. Its main purpose is to isolate your entire Python environment into a virtual one, including all the Python modules that you use. This has two major benefits. The first is that sometimes you need to run two different Python projects on the same machine, but each project requires a different version of the same library. Using `VirtualEnv`, each project would have its own virtualized version of the Python setup, so it becomes trivial to install two different version of the same library. The second advantage is that your environment becomes more portable, and in theory, it is easy to migrate an application running in a `VirtualEnv` environment to another machine that has `VirtualEnv` installed.

The `VirtualEnv` environment is widely used for Python development, especially for Flask. My decision to not include it in the main body of the book proved highly controversial with the reviewers, many of whom felt that the book was incomplete without it. I decided not to include it for two reasons. The first is that while I was learning Flask, I read many tutorials and examples, which included VirtualEnv. I always found the extra work needed for the setup and explanation of `VirtualEnv` and virtual environments in general to be distracting from the main content of the tutorial (namely, using Flask). The second reason is that I still often do not use it in the Flask projects I build today. If you're not running old software that depends on a particular version of a particular library, then installing useful Python libraries system-wide so that they can be used by all your Python applications is convenient. Also, sometimes, VirtualEnv can just become a mission without providing any value.

Of course, you may already have your own opinion on VirtualEnv, in which case you're welcome to go along with it. There's nothing stopping anyone from building any of the projects in this book in a `VirtualEnv` environment if they have a little experience. If you have not used it before, it's well worth looking at. You can install it through pip and try it out to take a look at exactly what it does and whether it can be of use in your particular scenario. You can read more about it and how to use it here:

```
http://docs.python-guide.org/en/latest/dev/virtualenvs/
```

Flask Blueprints

Perhaps the biggest feature of Flask that we haven't mentioned in this book is Flask Blueprints. You must have noted after building three Flask applications that certain patterns crop up time and again. Repeated code is bad code even over a number of different applications; if you find a better way to do something or need to make some changes for an update, you don't want to make the same change across several applications.

Blueprints provide a way to specify patterns for a Flask application. If you have several applications that use the same code to return templates or connect to a database, you can rather write this common code in a blueprint and then have all the applications register the blueprint.

You can read more about Flask Blueprints, take a look at examples, and learn how to get started with using them at `http://flask.pocoo.org/docs/0.10/blueprints/`.

Flask extensions

We looked at quite a few different Flask extensions over the course of our three projects. However, because of the educational focus of the book, we chose to write some code from scratch that may be better off using existing extensions. (Generally when developing, we want to avoid reinventing the wheel. If someone else has already put thought into solving a problem and provided a well-developed and well-maintained solution, it's better to use their offerings than to try and create our own.) Of special interest are the extensions we could use to make our user account system simpler and more powerful and those that offer us a more abstract way to talk to our database.

Flask-SQLAlchemy

Another controversial decision in this book was of not introducing the Flask-SQLAlchemy extension along with MySQL. SQLAlchemy provides a SQL toolkit and ORM to make it easier and more secure to interact with SQL databases from a Python environment. ORM provides another layer of abstraction between the web application and database. Instead of having to write the SQL code directly, one can make calls to a database using Python objects, which ORM will then translate to and from SQL. This makes the database easier to write and maintain and also more secure (ORM is normally very good at mitigating against any potential SQL injection vulnerabilities). The reasons to omit it were similar to the reasons to omit VirtualEnv — when learning, too many layers of abstraction can do more harm than good, and it's always advantageous to have first-hand experience with the problems that tools solve before blindly using the tools directly.

For any Flask application that uses a MySQL database, such as our Crime Map project, it is highly recommendable to use ORM, as with most Flask extensions. Flask-SQLAlchemy is just a wrapper for an existing non-Flask-specific library. You can find out more about SQLAlchemy at `http://www.sqlalchemy.org/` and a comprehensive guide to Flask-SQLAlchemy, including common usage patterns, here:

```
http://flask.pocoo.org/docs/0.10/patterns/sqlalchemy/
```

Flask MongoDB extensions

There are several Flask extensions that are intended to make interfacing with MongoDB easier. As MongoDB is relatively new, none of these has reached quite the maturity or is in as wide use as SQLAlchemy; therefore, if you intend to use one of them, it is recommended that you examine each to decide which one best suits your needs.

Flask-MongoAlchemy

Perhaps the most similar to SQLAlchemy (and not just by name) is Flask-MongoAlchemy. Similarly to SQLAlchemy, MongoAlchemy is not Flask-specific. You can read more about the main project here at `http://www.mongoalchemy.org`. Flask-MongoAlchemy is a Flask wrapper for MongoAlchemy, which you can read more about here:

```
http://pythonhosted.org/Flask-MongoAlchemy
```

Flask-PyMongo

A thinner wrapper to MongoDB that is closer to using PyMongo directly as we did in our third project is Flask-PyMongo. Unlike MongoAlchemy, this does not provide an ORM equivalent; instead, it simply provides a way of connecting to MongoDB through PyMongo using syntax that is more consistent with the way Flask usually handles external resources. You can have a quick introduction to Flask-PyMongo on its GitHub page here:

```
https://github.com/dcrosta/flask-pymongo
```

Flask-MongoEngine

Yet another solution to using Flask in conjunction with MongoDB is MongoEngine (`http://mongoengine.org`). This is notable because it integrates with WTForms and Flask-Security, which we'll discuss in the following sections. You can read more about the Flask-specific extension for Mongo Engine at `https://pypi.python.org/pypi/flask-mongoengine`.

Flask-Mail

If we wanted to implement an automatic e-mail sending solution, such as that described earlier in this chapter, a helpful extension would be Flask-Mail. This allows you to easily send e-mails from your Flask application along with handling attachments and bulk mailing. As mentioned before, these days, it's worthwhile to consider using a third-party service such as Amazon's SES instead of sending e-mails yourself. You can read more about Flask-Mail at `http://pythonhosted.org/Flask-Mail`.

Flask-Security

The final extension we'll talk about is Flask-Security. This extension is notable because a large part of it is actually built by combining other Flask extensions. In some ways, it departs from the Flask philosophy of doing as little as possible to be useful and allowing the user full freedom for custom implementations. It assumes that you are using one of the database frameworks we described, and it pulls together functionality from Flask-Login, WTForms, Flask-Mail, and other extensions to attempt to make building user account control systems as straightforward as possible. If we used this, we would have had a centralized way of handling registering accounts, logging in accounts, encrypting passwords, and sending e-mails instead of having to implement each part of the login system separately. You can read more about Flask-Security here:

```
https://pythonhosted.org/Flask-Security
```

Other Flask extensions

There are many Flask extensions, and we've only highlighted the ones that we think would be generally applicable in many web development scenarios here. Of course, when you develop a unique web application, you'll have much more specific needs, and chances are that someone has already had a similar need and created a solution. You can find an extensive (but not complete) list of Flask extensions here:

```
http://flask.pocoo.org/extensions
```

Expanding your web development knowledge

In this book, we focused on backend development—that done through Python or Flask. A large part of developing web applications is building a frontend that is powerful, aesthetically pleasing, and intuitive to use. Although we provided a solid grounding in HTML, CSS, and JavaScript, each of these topics is big enough for its own book, and many such books exist.

JavaScript is perhaps the most important of the three. Known as the "language of the web", it has gained steadily in popularity over the last few years (although, as with all languages, it has its fair share of critics). There are many frameworks for building JavaScript-intensive web applications (so many, in fact, that their sheer number and the frequency of new ones being released has become a topic of humor among developers). We introduced Bootstrap in this book, which includes basic JavaScript components, but for more heavily interactive applications, there exist larger frameworks. Three of the more popular frontend frameworks include AngularJS (built by Google), React.js (built by Facebook), and Ember.js (sponsored by a variety of corporations, including Yahoo!). Learning any of these frameworks or one of the many others will definitely help you build larger and more complicated web applications with richer frontends.

JavaScript is also no longer limited to the frontend, and many modern web applications are built using JavaScript on the server side as well. A common way to achieve this is through Node.js, which could have fully replaced Python and Flask in any of the projects we built.

HTML5 and CSS3 have grown far more powerful than the older technologies they evolved from. Earlier, there was a clear division of labor, with HTML for content, CSS for styling, and JavaScript for actions. Now, there is far more overlap between the capabilities of the three technologies, and some impressive and interactive applications are built using only HTML5 and CSS3 without the normal addition of JavaScript.

Summary

In this appendix, we looked forwards and pointed out some key areas and resources that will help you move beyond what was covered in detail in this book. We covered these areas in three topics: the projects we worked on in this book, the Flask resources that we didn't use, and web development in general.

This brings us to the end. However, the world of technology is so vast and so rapidly moving that, hopefully, this is more of a beginning than an end. As you continue your adventures, learning more about life, Python, and web development, I hope that some of the ideas presented in this book stay with you.

Index